D0792013

The
Woman's Day
Book of Weekend Crafts

The
Woman's Day
Book of Weekend Crafts

More Than 100 Quick-to-Finish Projects
by the Editors of *Woman's Day*

Houghton Mifflin Company   Boston   1978

57446

Library of Congress Cataloging in Publication Data
Main entry under title:

The Woman's day book of weekend crafts.

   1. Handicraft.   I. Woman's day.
TT157.W613 1978   745.5   77-15496
ISBN 0-395-26284-4

Printed in the United States of America

A 10 9 8 7 6 5 4 3 2 1

Contents

Introduction

With a very few exceptions, all of the projects in this book can be finished, if not in one sitting, at least in one specific span of time — an evening, a Saturday, or a weekend. The exceptions, which were too good to exclude, may take as long as a three- or four-day weekend. So, if you are the kind of person who likes to finish what you start — or if you want a break from that endless crocheted bedspread — or if you want to try something you never did before — or if you just want to spend a creative weekend at home, this book is designed for you.

Although the first criterion we set for these crafts was that they could be finished in a short period of time, the second (and more important) was that the finished pieces had to be something you would be proud to own, or give, or even sell.

With this in mind, you may be surprised as you look through the book at what seem to be some fairly complicated or elaborate projects. But there's a trick to becoming a weekend craftsperson. The trick — and it is a simple one — is to pick your project and then make a *complete* list of the materials and tools, if any, needed to complete it. If you do all of your shopping or collecting beforehand, you will be surprised at how much you can actually accomplish in a short span of time. But be thorough. Go over the list of materials needed a couple of times; you don't want to find yourself at two o'clock on a Sunday afternoon without the right color of wool or the right piece of wood.

If you aren't experienced in following directions, here's another tip: There is nothing more discouraging or confusing than trying to read through directions all at once. Don't try it. Directions aren't meant to be read *through*, they're meant to be followed. So read one step, follow it, and then go on to the next. "Step-by-step directions" is a phrase you've heard many times but probably never analyzed. Step by step is how to go about making the crafts in this book.

We had a good time making these selections, trying to pick the very cream of the crafts that have appeared in *Woman's Day* over the past few years. Now we wish you many happy evenings and weekends of transforming dry directions into colorful, exciting, handmade objects.

The Editors of Woman's Day

CRAFTS
FOR THE HOUSE

Nostalgic Picture: Country Idyll

Do as great-grandmother did — use your needle and sewing scraps to create heirloom art.

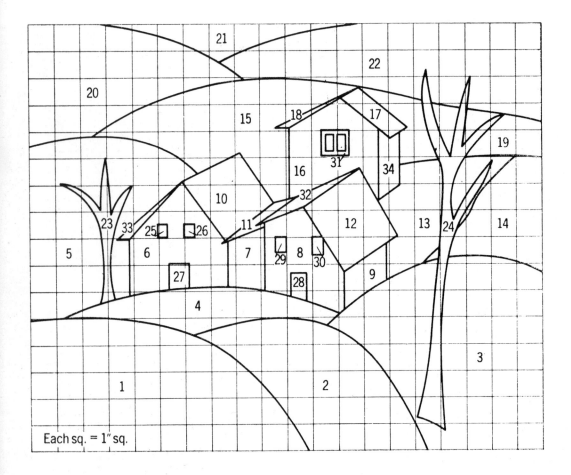

Each sq. = 1" sq.

Picture Size: 16″ x 20″.

Materials:
burlap for background, 18″ x 22″ plus margins for mounting
12″ square each red calico, multicolor floral print, miniature
   and ¼″ black and white gingham, black felt
scraps of black and white block print, houndstooth check,
   peasant print, red plaid
thread
a drawing board or plain board 24″ x 36″
thumbtacks
pins
16″ x 20″ hardboard
white glue

Enlarge design according to directions on page 175; transfer to burlap with dressmaker's carbon; go over lines with pen or pencil. Make an extra tracing of trees, roofs, and windows; cut from black felt and put aside. Cut apart landscape design for patterns. Follow photograph for colors and cut fabrics, adding ⅝″ allowance for turn-under; number pieces on back as in diagram. Press patches and burlap; tack top edge of burlap to board.

Pin and sew fabric pieces to burlap in numerical order, turning under allowance and clipping on curves; use any hemming stitch. Glue on felt pieces. Press and steam picture.

Glue to hardboard; insert in frame.

Stained-Glass Lamp Base

Although the working time on this project isn't long, you will have to allow for drying time. To get a head start, wash and dry the bottle beforehand. You can add the socket and the shade later, if necessary, but have them on hand before you begin so this won't be another "unfinished" project.

Materials:
   gallon-size light green or clear glass bottle or jug
   tube of liquid steel, from craft or hobby shop
   glass stain — yellow, red, green, and blue, from craft or
      hobby shop
   black crayon
   glass cleaner or ammonia
   lamp kit, from hardware store
   lamp shade

Remove label and clean jug thoroughly with mild soap and water solution; let dry. Before applying the liquid steel for leading, refer to photograph and with black crayon mark guidelines for stained-glass areas. Following manufacturer's directions, begin squeezing out liquid steel over crayon guidelines. Set off larger areas first, then break up smaller spaces. Allow leading to dry thoroughly. If lines are not thick enough, go over again; let dry. Clean any fingerprints from glass areas with the glass cleaner or ammonia. Following manufacturer's directions and referring to photograph for color guide, paint stained-glass areas with glass stains and a small brush. Let dry.

Follow manufacturer's directions to install lamp socket with cord and plug in neck of bottle. Add shade.

Here's a beautiful use for a gallon wine bottle or other jug after you've
used up the contents.

Ticktacktoe Potholder

The photograph shows two potholders so you can see both sides.

Size: 6½" square.

Materials:

    Coats and Clark's Speed-Cro-Sheen, 1 (100-yard) skein each white and black

    steel crochet hook No. 2, *or the size that will give you the correct gauge*

    tapestry needle

Gauge: 6 sc = 1"; 13 rows = 2"

Note: Potholder is made of two squares, one white and one black, embroidered, then crocheted together.

Square: Starting at one edge with white, ch 37 to measure 6½". **1st row:** Sc in 2nd ch from hook and in each ch across (36 sc); ch 1, turn. **2nd row:** Sc in each sc across; ch 1, turn. Repeat 2nd row until piece is square. Break off.

    Make another square with black.

    Using tapestry needle with Speed-Cro-Sheen and following photograph for placement, chain-stitch ticktacktoe design on white square with black and on black square with white.

    Working through both squares with black, sc evenly around edges of squares to join, working 3 sc at each corner and making hanging loop at center of one side as follows: Sc in center st, ch 15, sc in same st as last sc.

Two Sets of Desk Accessories

Brilliant splashes of flowered chintz coordinate this charming desk set. Only the accordion file was purchased before being covered.

GENERAL DIRECTIONS

You will need the following *tools:*
  metal-edged ruler and triangle
  mat knife
  white glue
  tongue depressor
  scissors
  wide, stiff brush for gluing

All items are constructed of $\frac{1}{16}$"-thick mat board. Never cut through more than one piece of board at a time. When greater thickness is required, cut several pieces from the board, then glue them together to desired thickness. (*Note:* Place weights on board to prevent warping.) Laminate these pieces first and let dry before constructing items. If desired, glue a strip of bond paper over the edges of the laminated pieces for smoothness.

To Make Box: Glue sides B and C to A (see Diagram 1), and, when dry, glue sides D and E to A, B, and C pieces (see Diagram 2). The white glue works best when thickened slightly; expose it to air for about an hour before using.

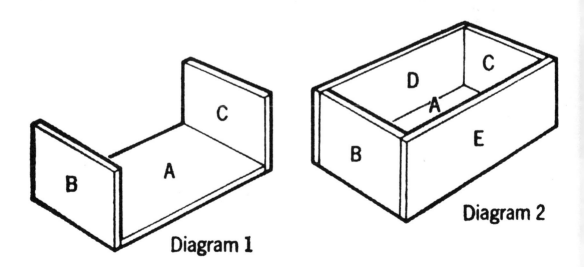

Diagram 1

Diagram 2

To Apply Covering Material: Dilute glue with water, if necessary, to enable smooth spreading. When fabric is used (as in chintz set), apply glue to the board; when paper is used (as in decorative-paper set), apply glue to the paper. Spread glue evenly over entire surface. After covering material is applied to board, smooth the material with tongue depressor to remove any air bubbles. (*Note:* You can use a piece of bond paper between covering material and tongue depressor to protect material.)

To Cover Flat Surface: Center and glue board to wrong side of covering material. Next, *miter corners* to remove excess bulk as in Diagram 3. Then fold material over edges of board and glue. Center and glue lining piece to uncovered section of board.

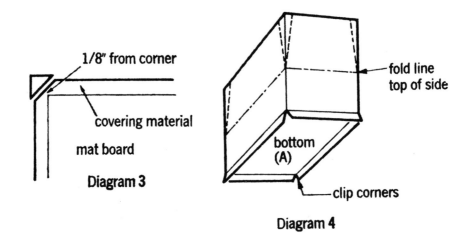

Diagram 3

Diagram 4

To Cover Box: Place side D on wrong side of material ½" from width edge and with bottom (A) ½" from a length edge. Turn box so that side B is on material, then continue rolling box across material covering sides E and C. Fold ½" excess at side over and let dry. Clip corners of excess fabric at bottom of box, turn under, and glue (see Diagram 4). Following Diagram 4, cut narrow triangles (broken lines) no wider than board thickness at top corners. Fold excess to inside of box and glue in place to form lining. Center and glue A lining pieces to both sides of bottom of box.

Materials:

1½ yards 45"-wide floral print chintz
1/16"-thick mat board, one piece each 22" x 30" and 30" x 40"
1¼ yards ⅜"-wide matching grosgrain ribbon
purchased accordion file measuring 5" x 11"
wooden spring-type clothespin
13⅝" x 17¼" blotter

See General Directions.

Blotter Holder: From mat board cut and laminate two pieces 14" x 17½". From chintz cut one piece 15½" x 19" for top and one 13½" x 17" for underside. Center and glue top piece in place.

From board cut two 4¼" squares, then cut squares in half diagonally to form four corner triangles. From chintz cut two 6" squares and two 3½" squares, then cut each square in half diagonally (eight triangles).

For each corner work as follows: Center and glue board triangle on wrong side of large chintz triangle. Fold fabric over long diagonal side and glue. Trim excess ends at fold to keep triangle shape, then miter right-angle corner *only*. Center and glue small lining triangle to board. Place covered triangle, lining side down, on top side of covered board, matching corner right angles. Fold remaining chintz edges to underside of covered board and glue.

After all corners are glued to board, center and glue lining piece to underside of board. Insert blotter.

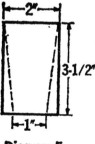

Diagram 5

Paper Clip: From board cut two pieces 2″ x 3½″. Following dimensions on Diagram 5, cut boards along broken lines. Following shape of boards, from chintz cut two top pieces, adding ¼″ on each side, and two lining pieces, subtracting ⅛″ on each side.

Cover boards. With thickened glue, attach clothespin to lining side of boards with pincher at narrow ends.

Letter Holder: From board cut six pieces 2″ x 7″ and laminate (A); cut three pieces 3″ x 7″ and laminate (B); cut three pieces 4″ - B″ and laminate (C). Following Diagram 1, assemble holder with glue.

From chintz cut piece 4″ x 8″ and glue to front (outside) of B, clipping at corner edges where A and B meet to insure smooth edges when folding around board. From chintz cut piece 5″ x 8″ and glue to back (outside) of C as for B. From chintz cut piece 2¼″ x 8¾″. Center this piece on underside of A and glue. Miter excess ends, then fold over A edges to top of A and glue.

Cut chintz lining pieces 3″ x 7″ (B) and 4″ x 7″ (C) and glue to inside of letter holder, extending each piece about ½″ onto top of A. Cut 1¾″ x 7″ piece of chintz and glue to top of A.

Two-Drawer Chest: For each drawer work as follows: From board cut one piece 2½″ x 4¾″ (A) and two pieces each 1½″ x 2½″ (B and C) and 1½″ x 4⅞″ (D and E). Construct drawer as a box. From chintz cut piece 4″ - 50″ and two (A lining) pieces 2½″ x 4¾″. Cover drawer, adding drawer-pull loop as follows: Cut 4″ length of ribbon, fold in half lengthwise, and, placing ends under A lining piece on box bottom, glue at center front. Make two drawers in this manner.

To make chest, work as follows: From board cut and laminate two pieces 1¹¹⁄₁₆″ x 5⅛″ (A); cut four pieces 1¹¹⁄₁₆″ x 3″ and laminate two pieces each (B and C); cut four pieces 3″ x 5⅜″, laminating and setting two pieces aside for D and laminating other two pieces for E. Construct partial box, omitting D. Work another partial box in same manner; then glue together with D between to form drawer partition of chest.

Cut piece of chintz 4″ x 19½″ and cover chest as for box, clipping at center partition for smooth edges when folding around board. Cut chintz strip 1″ x 5⅛″ and cover partition edge. Cut and apply 3¾″ x 5⅜″ back lining piece. (*Note:* Inside of chest is not lined.) Insert drawers in chest.

An unusual corklike paper makes an effective covering for this quite
different set of desk accessories.

Pencil (or Flower) Holder: From board and chintz cut one piece each 2″ square (A), two pieces each 2″ x 3½″ (B and C), and two pieces each 2⅛″ x 3½″ (D and E). Glue chintz to one side of each board and construct box so that covered sides are interior of box. Cut piece of chintz 4½″ x 9¼″ and cover as for outside of box. Cut 2⅛″ square of chintz and cover bottom. Insert dried flowers or use as pencil holder.

Accordion File: From board cut two pieces 5¼″ x 11½″ for front and back facings on file. Cut two pieces of chintz 6¼″ x 12½″; cover one side of each board, folding excess over edges. Cut strips ½″ x 11″ from chintz and cover top edge of each file section. Cut two pieces of chintz 5″ x side width of file plus 1″ and glue in place. Glue uncovered sides of boards to front and back of file. Cut 1 yard of ribbon; center and glue to bottom of file.

DECORATIVE PAPER DESK SET

Materials:
> 2½ square yards decorative paper such as wrapping or gift paper
> 1/16″-thick mat board, two pieces 30″ x 40″
> 13¾″ x 16½″ blotter
> 3½″-long golf pencils
> 4″ x 6″ sheets memo paper

See General Directions.

Blotter Holder: From mat board cut piece 14″ x 20″. From paper cut piece 15″ x 19″, center and cover top of board, folding paper over long edges of board.

For each side panel cut board 2½″ x 14″; cut paper 3¾″ x 15″. Center panel on paper and glue to top only. Fold paper over one long edge and glue. Cut paper 2″ x 13½″·for lining and glue to uncovered side of panel. Miter two corners opposite folded edge, leaving ¼″ paper at corners. Line up uncovered long edges of panel to sides of board, fold paper to back of board and glue. Cut paper 13¾″ x 19¾″ and glue to back of board. Insert blotter.

Mail-to-Answer Box with Lid: Cut three pieces board 9″ x 12½″ (A) and six pieces each 2″ x 9″ (B and C) and 2″ x 12⅞″ (D and E). Laminate three pieces for bottom and each side.

Construct box. From paper cut piece 5" x 46" and two lining pieces 9" x 12½"; cover box.

For lid cut and laminate three pieces 8¾" x 12¼". From paper cut one piece each 10¼" x 13¾" and 8½" x 12"; cover board. For knob cut and laminate eight 1¾" squares. Cut paper 4" square and cover knob in same manner as for box, rolling it across paper. Miter all corners and glue down sides. Finish top edge (A) with lining piece. Center and glue knob to lid.

Miniature Pencil Holder: Holder is unlined. Make box with colored mat board, constructing it so that color is on inside of box. From board cut one piece 1⅛" square (A), two pieces 1⅛" x 1¾" (B and C), and two pieces 1¼" x 1¾" (D and E). Construct box. From paper cut piece 2½" x 6" and a 1⅛" square; cover box.

Sharpen pencils. For each pencil cut paper strip measuring circumference of pencil plus ⅛" x pencil length. Cover by rolling pencil in glued paper.

Stationery Holder: From board cut six pieces 3⅛" x 4⅝". Following broken line on Diagram 6, cut away one corner of each piece. Laminate three pieces each for B and C. Cut and laminate three pieces each 3⅛" x 10" (A), 2¾" x 10⅜" (D), and 4⅝" x 10⅜" (E). Construct box.

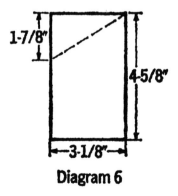

Diagram 6

From paper cut piece 4" x 11¼" and cover outer side of D, carefully mitering corners where angled sides meet. Cut piece 5¾" x 11¼" and cover E in same manner. Following shape of B and C, adding ½" at top and lower edges, cut two pieces and glue to outer side of B and C. Following shape of same pieces, adding ¼" at each side edge and lower edge, cut two pieces and glue to inside of B and C. Cut piece 2¾" x 10" and line D and cut piece 4¾" x 10" and line E. Cut two pieces 3⅛" x 10" and line both sides of A.

Three-Compartment Organizer: From board cut two pieces 2½" x 4¾" (A) and laminate; cut four pieces each 1½" x 2½" (B and C) and 1½" x 5" (D and E) and laminate pairs. Construct box. Make two more boxes in same manner, then glue boxes together along D and E sides as in photograph.

Cut piece of paper 3¾" x 27" and cover box, carefully clipping self-lining sections at compartment partitions. From paper cut two pieces 3¾" x 4¾" and cover partitions. Cut three pieces 2½" x 4¾" and cover inside bottom of each compartment. Cut paper 4⅞" x 8⅛" and cover bottom of box.

Memo-Paper Dispenser Box: This box holds 4" x 6" sheets of paper.

From board cut three pieces each 4⅛" x 6⅛"(A) and 1¼" x 4⅛" (B); cut six pieces 1¼" x 6½" (D and E). Laminate three matching pieces of each to make bottom, sides, and one end. For side C cut three rectangles measuring 1¼" x 2", then cut each piece in half diagonally. Glue the triangles together in groups of three to form the two C pieces. Construct box following photograph for C side.

From paper cut piece 3½" x 23" and cover box, carefully trimming excess when lining C pieces. Cut piece 4" x 6" and line inside bottom of box. Cut piece 4⅜" x 6⅜" and cover bottom.

Woven Paper Basket with Lid

Ordinary newspaper is the material for this useful, pretty embroidery basket.

Materials:
  12 sheets standard-size (23″ x 29″) newspaper
  white glue
  brush for glue
  spring-type clothespins
  brass spray paint
  raw-umber acrylic paint (optional)

Cut newspaper sheets in half at center fold. Fold pieces in half lengthwise and cut again. Fold each quarter piece ¾″ from a long edge several times to make strips, brushing glue along edges of first and last folds. Make twenty-four folded strips for basket and twenty-three for lid and handle.

To weave bottom of basket, cross two strips at their centers and at right angles; glue at overlap. Add a third strip parallel to and ⅛″ away from top strip and under bottom strip; glue at overlap. Add a fourth strip parallel to single strip under last strip and over the other; glue at two overlaps. Continue weaving strips in all directions, keeping woven section square, until twenty strips are in place (ten strips in each direction).

For basket walls, weave a strip along one side ¼″ away from last strip, leaving short piece at starting end and longer piece at other end; glue at each overlap. Repeat with second strip along opposite side. Hold strips in place with clothespins. When dry, bend woven parts of strips up into walls, turning corners to weave adjacent walls with long ends. Weave and glue third and fourth sides; hold with clothespins. Cut ends of strips so they abut inside basket; glue and hold with clothespins. Repeat for second row of wall. To finish off rim, bend inside vertical strips out and outside strips in. Fold down and cut at bottom edge of top row of wall; glue and hold with clothespins until dry.

For lid, follow procedure to make basket, using two strips for a single-row wall and saving one strip for handle. Check lid size against basket as you weave to make lid slightly larger, adjusting spacing between strips by eye. Cut strip ends even around rim, fold to inside, and glue. Bend each end of strip for handle back and forth four times into accordion pleats, gluing each fold. Clamp folds with clothespins until dry. Glue handle to center of lid.

To finish basket, brush undiluted glue over all surfaces; let dry. Spray-paint brass; let dry. If desired, thin raw-umber acrylic with water and brush into crevices of basket to antique it; let dry.

Early American Fruit Box

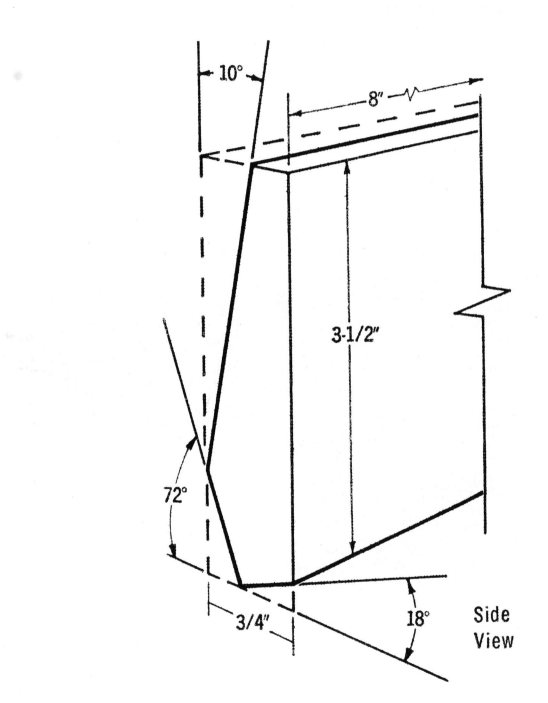

10°

8" ⌇

3-1/2"

72°

3/4"

18°

Side
View

Materials:
    3' length 1 x 4 and 1' length 1 x 10 pine stock
    twelve ¾" x No. 4 flathead wood screws
    white glue
    pine stain
    low-luster varnish
    paste wax

Before cutting sides, prepare a 3' length 1 x 4 pine stock. (The actual width must be an even ¾" thick.) Following pattern for profile of sides, transfer to pine. Mark and cut bottom edges; then, following pattern, taper board as indicated. Round top edges well; cut pine length into four 8" side pieces.

Cut 9½"-square bottom from 1 x 10 pine. Center and mark position for sides on underside of bottom (sides will just touch at corners). Predrill two screw holes for each side in bottom and sides. Countersink bottom. Round edges of bottom. Glue sides in place and fasten with screws.

To finish, sand box, then apply pine stain to all surfaces. When dry, finish with polyurethane varnish and paste wax.

"Wrought-Iron" Accessories

A rack for pots and pans, a trivet, and a candle sconce — no one would dream they were made, easily, of aluminum.

If you can swing a hammer and do a little painting, you can fashion these authentic-looking "wrought-iron" accessories. The stock aluminum bar is far easier to work with than wrought iron, and a ball-peen hammer adds deceptive texture. With a coating of flat black paint you can fool anyone.

GENERAL DIRECTIONS

Note: We used aluminum bar and rod to make our "wrought-iron" accessories. Aluminum bar and rod are purchased in 6' lengths and are available from most hardware, building-supply, and metal-supply stores. You will not need special tools to work with them or have to do any welding or brazing. Basic techniques for making the accessories follow.

Texturing: To look like wrought iron, aluminum rod and bar must be textured before cutting or bending to shape. Use a ball-peen hammer on rod and on both faces of bar, distributing marks fairly evenly. Texturing can be as heavy or light as desired. Blunt corners and distress edges in many places to complete the texturing.

Bending: It is generally easier to work with a long length of aluminum than with a short piece. After being bent, the piece is cut to size. However, the scrolls for the candle sconce and trivet must be cut to size first, then bent. Use vise-grip pliers to assist bending.

Five basic bends were used for the accessories shown:

1. The *long curve* used for semicircles on pot rack. Clamp one end of aluminum bar in vise, then gently bend bar by hand with thumbs inside curvature. If bar begins to develop stress peaks, smooth them out by working on other side of curve, placing thumbs on each side of peak. Continue to bend. Frequently check your bend against the pattern. When satisfied with curve, trim to exact size with a hacksaw as described under "Cutting."

2. The *sharp bend* used for one end of hooks on pot rack (see detail). Mark exact location of bend on aluminum and clamp bar in vise at this point. Pull bar by hand and use short blows of hammer just above bend to keep it as angular as possible. Move piece up in vise and continue to make bend. When bend is closed enough that sides fit in vise, insert entire hook in vise

A planter and a come-and-get-it mealtime triangle with its own striker.

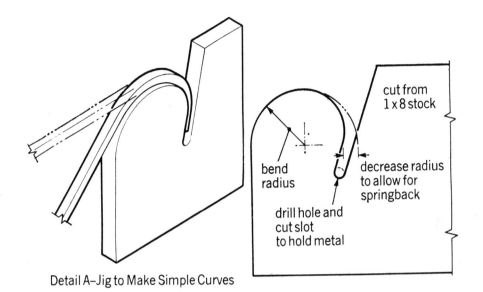

cut from
1 x 8 stock

bend
radius

decrease radius
to allow for
springback

drill hole and
cut slot
to hold metal

Detail A–Jig to Make Simple Curves

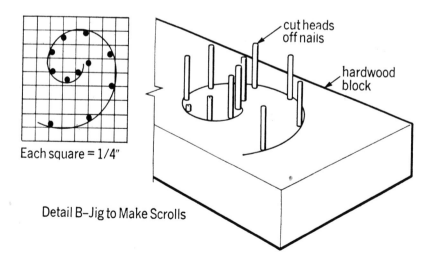

Each square = 1/4"

cut heads
off nails

hardwood
block

Detail B–Jig to Make Scrolls

and tighten. So that hook will not close fully, slip a piece of ⅛"-thick bar inside bend. Remove hook from vise and cut to size.

3. The *intermediate bend* used for triangle on dinner gong. For this bend, make a jig from a length of 1" pine or hardwood rounded on one end. Place jig and aluminum bar in a vise and tighten. Bend aluminum against rounded end of pine.

4. A *simple curve* can be made by using the jig shown in Detail A. The hanger bracket for the planter and the vertical support of the candle sconce both use this curve. The jig curve (radius) should always be slightly smaller (tighter) than the desired bend because the metal springs back slightly when released from jig. (Metal can be pulled open if jig curve is too tight.)

5. Jig for *scrolls* is hardwood block with nails partially driven in (see Detail B). The nailheads are first cut off with a hacksaw, and pilot holes for nails are drilled inside scroll guideline. Place additional headless nails at the beginning of scroll spiral to hold the aluminum bar or rod that is fitted between them.

If you do not want to make your own jigs for the simple curve and scrolls, you can order a *scroll former* from Creative Metalcraft, Dept. WD, 1083 Bloomfield Avenue, West Caldwell, N.J. 07006. Cost is $9.95, postpaid.

Cutting: Mark cutting line in pencil on aluminum bar. Securely clamp bar in a vise or use C-clamps to hold bar against solid work surface. Using a hacksaw with fine-tooth blade, cut bar. (*Note:* Hacksaw cuts on forward stroke. Do not force cutting, but cut with a steady, even stroke at a low angle.) File cut ends to remove all burrs and sharp edges.

Fastening: We used aluminum nails as rivets to join some pieces because they are easier to buy. Steel nails can be substituted. Drill matching holes as indicated on Detail C and on the assembly diagrams, using a bit that is the same diameter as the nail. Cut nails ⅛" longer than the combined thicknesses of pieces to be joined. Insert nail through holes, then, with nailhead resting on vise, anvil, or metal plate, flatten the protruding ⅛" against the aluminum bar with a ball-peen hammer.

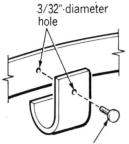

3/32"-diameter
hole

1-1/2" common aluminum
nail, cut 1/8" longer than
total thickness of
pieces being riveted

Detail C–Rivet Assembly

To fasten scrolls of the candle sconce to the vertical support and each other, use single or double wrappings of soft steel wire as shown in Detail D. Twist loose ends together; flatten at back.

wrap wire, twist
ends and hammer
flat

double
wrap

single
wrap

Detail D–Wire Wrapping

Finishing: Wipe each assembled piece with a cloth dipped in lacquer thinner and dry with another soft, clean cloth. Spray-paint piece with a flat back paint with rust retardant for metal; allow to dry overnight. Spray a second coat on piece; let dry. If paint chips later, respray piece and let dry.

POT RACK

Size: Approximately 15½" x 8" x 11½".

Materials:

    two 6' lengths ⅛" x 1" aluminum bar
    6' length ¼"-diameter aluminum rod
    1½" aluminum common nails or ⅞" aluminum roofing nails
    three 1" x 1" corner braces
    flat black spray paint for metal

Texture both lengths of aluminum bar as described in General Directions. Using dimensions on diagram, make a pattern for the semicircles on brown wrapping paper. Cut two pieces of aluminum bar slightly longer than pattern. Bend both pieces into long curves as described in General Directions. Cut pieces to size and assemble for frame as shown with two 1" x 1" corner braces. Use half the pattern to make two quarter-circles; bend and roughly cut pieces to size. Rivet quarter-circle pieces to frame, attaching top edges only, with 1" x 1" corner braces as shown; trim flush with edges of frame.

Cut pieces for scrolls, then bend to shape as described in General Directions, or use a scroll former. Cut scrolls and attach to frame with nail rivets. Make as many hooks as desired from ¼" rod, following General Directions for sharp bends and simple curves. Finish and paint rack with flat black paint.

Pothook Detail

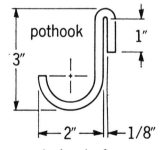

make hooks from
1/4" aluminum rod

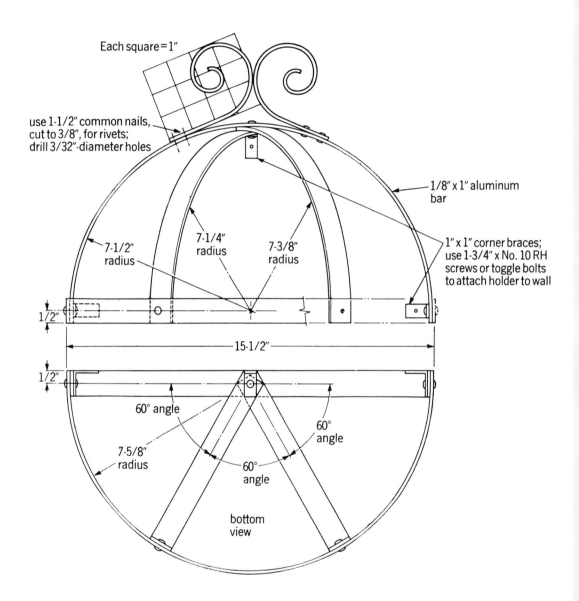

Each square = 1″

use 1-1/2″ common nails,
cut to 3/8″, for rivets;
drill 3/32″-diameter holes

1/8″ x 1″ aluminum
bar

7-1/2″
radius

7-1/4″
radius

7-3/8″
radius

1″ x 1″ corner braces;
use 1-3/4″ x No. 10 RH
screws or toggle bolts
to attach holder to wall

1/2″

15-1/2″

1/2″

60° angle

60°
angle

7-5/8″
radius

60°
angle

bottom
view

TRIVET

Size: 6″ x 10″.

Materials:
   two 6′ lengths ⅛″ x ¾″ aluminum bar
   1½″ aluminum common nails or ⅞″ aluminum roofing nails
   flat black spray paint for metal

Enlarge pattern for trivet (see directions for enlarging patterns on page 175). Texture aluminum bar as described in General Directions. Cut a 34″ length of aluminum bar for trivet frame, then mark center point of piece with pencil. At each end of length bend scrolls for fishtail as described in General Directions. Make a sharp bend at marked center point of length so that the angle matches pattern for fish head. Continue to bend long curves for body. Drill hole for rivet through center of tail as indicated and fasten with a nail rivet.

For legs, make intermediate bends in ends of remaining aluminum lengths and cut as indicated on pattern. Drill holes in legs and frame as shown and attach legs with nail rivets.

Following pattern, cut aluminum for body scrolls. Bend pieces to fit within frame. Drill holes to attach scrolls to frame with nail rivets. Finish and paint assembled trivet; let dry.

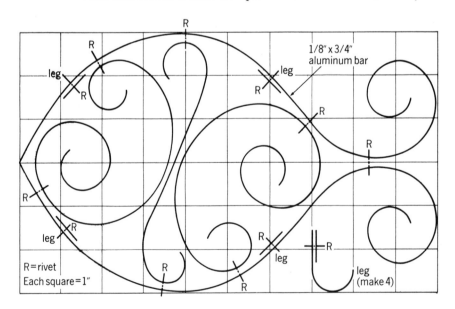

CANDLE SCONCE

Size: 20″ long.

Materials:

   3′ length ⅜″ x ⅜″ aluminum bar
   6′ length ¼″-diameter aluminum rod
   soft steel wire about $\frac{1}{16}$″ in diameter
   metal candle cup with bobeche, available at craft and
      hobby-supply stores, or a candle cup and bobeche with
      stand, available at variety stores
   ½″ x No. 6 or No. 8 self-tapping sheet-metal screw
   flat black spray paint for metal

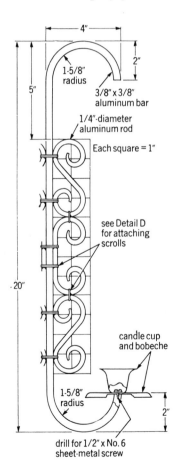

Cut ⅜" aluminum bar to 30" for vertical support. Make jig as shown in Detail A, page 35, referring to General Directions. Use jig to bend a simple curve at each end of bar. Trim 1" from each curved end.

Make patterns for scrolls and cut a piece of aluminum rod ¾" shorter than finished scroll length. Hammer ends of each rod on a metal plate, vise, or anvil to ⅛" thickness or until they fit between the holding nails of jig. (*Note:* Flattening the ends causes rod to stretch ¾".) Referring to General Directions for scrolls, bend half the rod at a time, reversing direction of bend for *S* curve and keeping same direction for *C* curve. Clamp the vertical support in a vise and attach the scrolls as shown in diagram, using soft wire. To attach candle cup, drill a pilot hole for ½" screw in lower end of vertical support and in candle cup through its rivet. (*Note:* If candle cup has stand, discard after drilling.) Fasten candle cup with screw. Finish and paint sconce; let dry.

HANGING PLANTER

Size: Will hold 6"-diameter pot.

Materials:
6' length ⅛" x ¾" aluminum bar
one pair 48"-long leather bootlaces
flat black spray paint for metal

Follow General Directions to texture a 55" aluminum bar. Mark and cut four 7¼" pieces for the plant holder. Align four pieces in a vise and clamp. Referring to diagram, mark positions for notches with pencil. Cut out all ⅜"-deep notches at one time, using a fine-tooth blade in a hacksaw. Remove pieces from vise and use long-nosed pliers to break away waste in cutout slots. Stack two hanger pieces and mark for ¼"-diameter holes as indicated. Clamp pieces together and drill holes. With file, round corners on hanger pieces and remove burrs or sharp edges around slots and holes.

Referring to General Directions for making long curves and intermediate bends, bend remaining 29" piece of aluminum for bracket. Trim bracket to length as indicated on diagram; drill mounting holes.

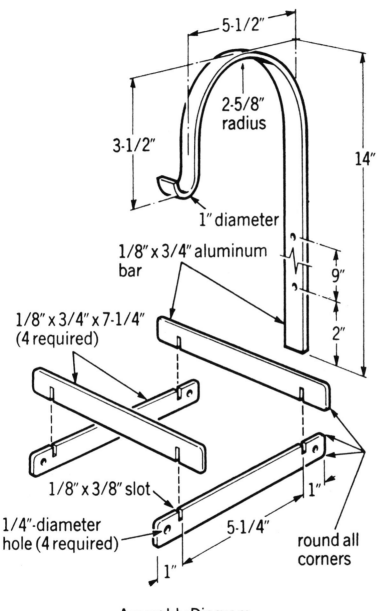

5-1/2"

2-5/8"
radius

3-1/2"

14"

1" diameter

1/8" x 3/4" aluminum
bar

9"

1/8" x 3/4" x 7-1/4"
(4 required)

2"

1/8" x 3/8" slot

1/4"-diameter
hole (4 required)

5-1/4"

1"

1"

round all
corners

Assembly Diagram
HANGING PLANTER

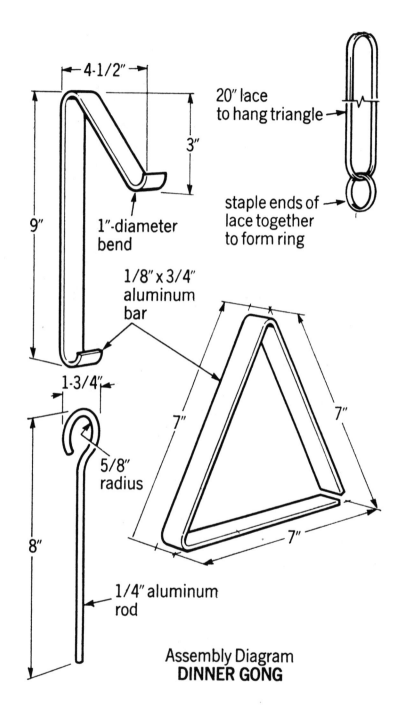

4-1/2"

3"

20" lace
to hang triangle →

9"

1"-diameter
bend

staple ends of →
lace together
to form ring

1/8" x 3/4"
aluminum
bar

1-3/4"

7"

7"

5/8"
radius

7"

8"

1/4" aluminum
rod

Assembly Diagram
DINNER GONG

Finish and paint all aluminum pieces; let dry. To hang planter, assemble holder as shown; cut laces to 36″ and tie in place. Mount bracket on wall with long screws directly into wall studs, or use toggle bolts if wall is plaster. Suspend holder from bracket as in photograph.

DINNER GONG

Materials:
    6′ length ⅛″ x ¾″ aluminum bar
    1½′ length ¼″-diameter aluminum rod
    48″-long leather bootlace
    desk stapler
    flat black spray paint for metal

Using the dimensions on diagram, draw pattern for both triangle and bracket on brown wrapping paper. Texture a 4′ length of bar as described in General Directions. Referring to instructions for making intermediate bends, bend triangle and bracket to shape; cut to size. Mark and drill holes for mounting bracket.

Bend ¼″ rod for striker as described for scrolls in General Directions, or use scroll former. When loop is formed, clamp piece in vise and open loop slightly with slip-joint pliers. Cut striker to size.

Finish all aluminum pieces as described in General Directions. For leather loops cut bootlace into one 4″ and one 20″ piece. Hold ends of shorter piece together and place on strike plate of stapler. Press stapler head firmly down on leather ends. Release and tightly clinch staple ends with pliers. Thread 20″ loop through leather ring and secure ends as described above. Mount bracket on wall with long screws directly into wall studs, or use toggle bolts if wall is plaster. Assemble gong as shown.

Bargello Lion Pillow

Each square = 1"

Here's an unusual pillow, quick to make in bargello stitch.

Size: Lion measures about 9½" wide x 12" tall.

Materials:
    12" x 15" piece mono (single-mesh) needlepoint canvas with
        10 meshes per inch
    12" x 15" piece yellow stretch knit for backing
    acrylic knitting worsted, 2 ounces yellow (color Y), 10 yards
        each gold (G) and brown (B), 3 yards orange (O), 1 yard
        each rust (R) and white (W)
    Dacron polyester for stuffing
    tapestry needle

To Prepare Canvas: Fold masking tape over edges to prevent raveling.

Enlarge pattern according to directions on page 175. Slide pattern under canvas and trace, using pencil or needlepoint marker.

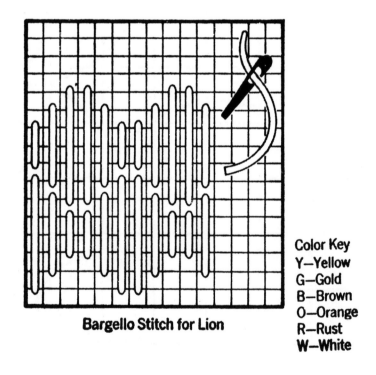

Bargello Stitch for Lion

Color Key
Y—Yellow
G—Gold
B—Brown
O—Orange
R—Rust
W—White

Yarn: Use two strands of yarn for bargello and satin stitches, one strand for all other stitches. Cut yarn in 10" lengths.

To Work Design: Work satin stitch in direction of markings for eyes, nose, and inner ears. Work a white French knot in each eye. Following bargello-stitch pattern, work lion's head and body.

Mane: With color G and tapestry needle sew 1½" yarn loops around lion's head. *Eyelashes:* With B make three ½" loops as for mane over each eye. Clip loops. *Tail:* Cut eighteen 8" strands Y and make braid. Cut thirty 6" strands G. Hold together and tie around center to make fat tassel. Sew to one end of braid.

Finishing: Block needlepoint and trim canvas, leaving ½" seam allowance all around stitching. Cut backing piece to same shape as canvas. With right sides facing, stitch needlepoint and backing together, leaving lower edge (including area around dot) open. Turn and stuff. Insert end of tail in opening at dot. Sew opening, catching tail in stitching.

Painted Stone Turtles

Here's an entertaining use for those pebbles you can't resist picking up at the beach.

Materials:

You will need smooth beach stones in assorted sizes, 1 for body and 1 for head of each turtle, 4 for each set of legs (choose stones that are in proportion and make sure that leg stones are fairly uniform so that turtles will be level), and 1 flat stone approximately 1¾" x 3" for stand; tiny conch shell to place with turtle on stand (see photograph); points of toothpicks for tails; waterproof markers in assorted colors; clear varnish; epoxy.

Following photograph, color body of each turtle as desired with markers and draw eyes and nose on head. Varnish all stones and let dry. Glue legs to body. When dry, glue on head, propping it to hold in position while drying. Color tip of toothpick for tail; cut to size and glue to underside of turtle.

To make turtle with stand, follow photograph for placement of shell and turtle; glue in place.

FLOWERS — FABULOUS FAKES

Fabric Anemones

Scraps of cloth and a few simple items are all you need to create the most exquisite fabric flowers. After you have completed your arrangement of anemones, you'll surely want to try other varieties. The principle is the same. Just follow our General Directions.

Materials:
    flower fabric — cotton voile or thin lining material, red, bright orange, and white for the petals; moss green for the leaves
    black and white pearlized artificial stamens
    $5/8$"-diameter dark blue buttons with 2 or 4 holes
    heavy craft glue
    sharp nail scissors
    No. 28-gauge covered white wire for petals
    No. 24-gauge covered green wire for leaves
    No. 18-gauge covered green wire for stems
    spool of very fine flexible wire
    floral tape
    chunks of plastic foam (optional)
    waxed paper

GENERAL DIRECTIONS

Petals and Leaves: Cut a length of No. 28 white wire and shape into desired petal shape, leaving a 2" tail of wire ends twisted together. Cut pieces of fabric into squares or rectangles slightly larger than wire petal frame. Squeeze out glue onto waxed paper, dip wire petal frame into glue, coating it completely, and press onto wrong side of a fabric piece. Continue making petals; allow to dry. With nail scissors carefully cut away excess fabric as close as possible to outside edge of wire frame. Using No. 24 green wire, follow same method to make leaves.

Assembling Flowers: Bunch petals for a single flower into a cluster with a small cluster of appropriate artificial stamens in center. Bind clusters securely with thin flexible wire. Cut a piece of No. 18 wire for stem the length appropriate for type of flower. Insert one end of stem wire into cluster. Begin wrapping bound part of clustered petals and stamens with floral tape as in photograph. Continue wrapping down stem, adding leaves at intervals along stem as you cover it. Shape petals and leaves with fingers as shown.

Arranging: Use a chunk of plastic foam in bottom of wide-mouth container or vase to help hold stems. Conceal foam with dry decorative moss or pebbles.

ANEMONES

Finished anemones measure about 3¼" in diameter. Referring to General Directions, make eight rounded petals and two or three slim, elongated leaves for each flower. For white at center of each petal cluster, cut a small triangular shape with one rounded side and glue on top of each petal near twisted wire ends of frame. Divide stamens into bunches of three for each hole in buttons. Cut off one pearl end of each stamen if they are double-ended, insert bunches into holes, and twist stamen ends together to hold on underside of button. Divide twenty more stamens into four bunches of five each. Arrange bunches around outer rim of button and bind securely with fine flexible wires to other stamen ends protruding from button. Assemble petals as described in General Directions. Cut a 10" or 12" stem from No. 18-gauge wire and insert in flower cluster. Wrap stem, adding leaves as described in General Directions. Shape finished flower as in photograph.

This makes a beautiful centerpiece for Easter. Start blowing out the eggs well in advance so you'll have enough shells for a whole bouquet of tulips by Easter time. These are truly lovely. Here's how you can go about turning ordinary eggshells into extraordinary tulips.

Materials:
    uncooked white and brown eggs
    needle
    cuticle scissors
    pastel tempera, acrylic paints, or Paas Easter Egg Coloring
    floral tape
    green crepe paper
    thin wire
    6 to 8 artificial stamens for each flower, available in most
        hobby and craft stores
    white glue
    small pebbles or a chunk of plastic foam

To blow out eggs, pierce a tiny hole in narrow end of egg with needle. At wider end, gently crack egg and chip away a larger hole for contents of egg to come out. Blow contents into bowl or plate.

With cuticle scissors, cut the eggshell at larger hole into tulip petals as in photograph. Carefully wash eggshells and allow to dry. Leave all of the brown shells and a few of the white ones unpainted. Color some of the white eggshells by thinning either pastel tempera or acrylic paints with water to a watercolor consistency; brush on and let dry (if using egg coloring, follow directions on package).

Cut thin wire into 6" to 8" pieces for stems; grouping six to eight stamens, wind one end of stem wire tightly around them. Following photograph, cut out bladelike leaves from crepe paper — about three for each tulip. Insert and pull tip of wire stem through tiny hole in tulip so that stamens are clustered inside tulip bowl. Dribble white glue around stamens to seal off hole and hold them in place. Wrap bare wire stem with floral tape, adding leaves as you wrap.

To arrange bouquet, insert stems into plastic foam or, if you have a smaller arrangement, use pebbles to keep stems upright in container.

Embroidered Daisies
in a Basket

Decorate a pillow, shirt, or jumper with our iron-on embroidered daisies, or put them on a background and frame them.

Size: Embroidered area is 8″ wide x 8¾″ deep.

Materials:
>   pale blue linenlike fabric for background
>   iron-on bonding fabric, 1 package each 6½″ x 14″ pieces white, dark green, and beige
>   8½-yard skeins 6-strand embroidery floss in the following colors: 3 skeins each tan, white, and dark green; 2 skeins shaded yellow
>   embroidery needle

The three-dimensional effect is achieved by cutting shapes from bonding fabric, binding them to background fabric or your garment, then embroidering over shapes.

Cut fabric for background. Whipstitch all edges to prevent raveling.

To Cut: Enlarge patterns on brown paper for daisies, leaves, and baskets according to directions on page 175. Use photograph as guide for arrangement or prepare a sketch of your own.

Using patterns, cut from bonding fabrics white petals for all the daisies, green leaf shapes (two pieces for each leaf), and beige strips (follow solid lines) for basket.

To Assemble and Bond: Working on ironing board, assemble all cutout pieces on background fabric as in photograph or following your sketch. Working from bottom up, arrange horizontal basket strips, daisy petals, and leaves, then cut ⅛″-wide green bonding-fabric strips for stems and place them among foliage. Following manufacturer's directions, use a dry iron to bind shapes to background. (*Note:* Test a scrap of iron-on fabric on scrap of background fabric to check correct temperature. Use a press cloth if background fabric tends to scorch.) With pencil, mark vertical lines on basket strips, following broken lines on pattern.

To Embroider: It is not necessary to use an embroidery hoop when working over bonded shapes, because the bonding fabric keeps the stitches flat and smooth. Try not to handle

62

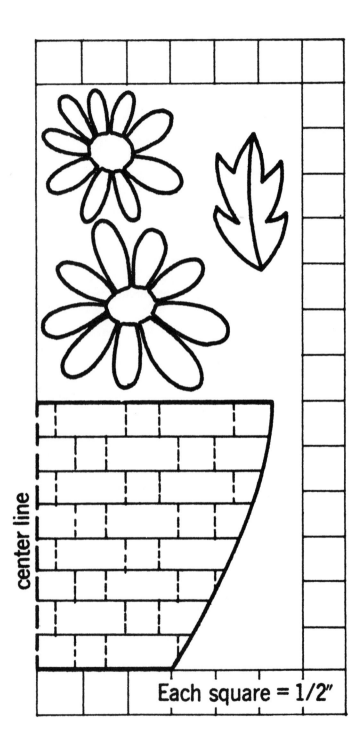

center line

Each square = 1/2"

bonded shapes too much as you work, in order to keep their crisp quality. Work with three strands floss throughout. Work satin stitch (see stitch diagram) over all bonded shapes, working darkest color (green) first, then tan, then white. For basket, alternate direction of satin stitch, vertically and horizontally, on each strip, inserting needle along pencil lines. Work daisy centers in clusters of French knots (see stitch diagram), using three strands shaded yellow.

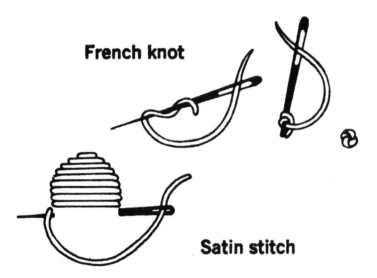

French knot

Satin stitch

Roses from Cans

These lovely flowers made from soft molded aluminum beverage cans are remarkably easy to make and offer a charming, everlasting floral decoration. (And what an elegant recycling project!) You start by opening up the cans and flattening them; then, using our patterns, cut out the flower-petal and leaf shapes with ordinary scissors. Petals are sprayed in shaded rose tones and curled around your finger or a dowel; leaves are sprayed green. Each flower is assembled by slipping the petal shapes on coat-hanger wire and securing with thin wire and glue.

Size: 3½" to 5½".

Materials:
> 12- and 16-ounce molded aluminum beverage cans (don't use the heavier-gauge metal cans)
> awl
> wire coat hangers
> sharp scissors
> long-nosed pliers
> wire cutters
> No. 20-gauge flexible wire
> black felt-tipped marker or china marker
> lightweight cardboard
> scrap ¼"-diameter dowel
> pigmented-shellac primer
> spray enamel in several colors
> quick-drying epoxy
> spray satin-finish varnish (optional)

Note: You will need two 16-ounce and three 12-ounce aluminum cans to make each rose.

All petals and leaves are cut from aluminum. Wash and dry cans. Use an awl to punch several small holes along top edge of can so that scissor blades can be inserted. Insert scissors and carefully cut off top, then cut down side and cut off rounded bottom. Flatten aluminum by pulling it over a table edge in the opposite direction of the natural roll.

Enlarge patterns on cardboard for all petals, calyx, and leaf cluster (see directions for enlarging patterns, page 175); cut out patterns. Using patterns and marking pen or china marker, trace one A (petal), one B (petal), two C's (petal), two D's

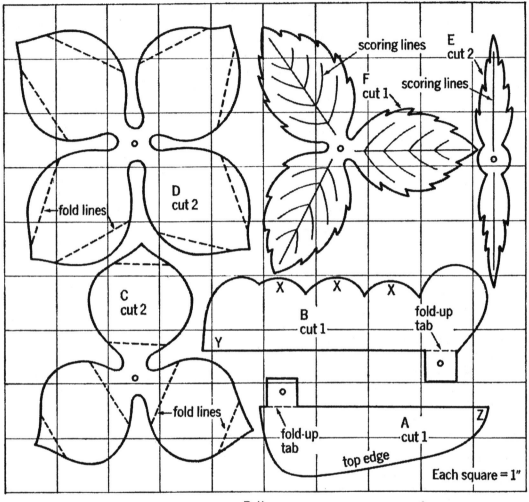

Patterns

(petal), two E's (calyx), and one F (leaf cluster) on aluminum;
cut out with sharp scissors. With hammer and awl, punch a
hole as indicated through all petal and leaf pieces.

Using scrap dowel, shape petals C and D along folded lines
indicated on patterns. Do *not* shape or roll up petals A and B at
this time. Sharpen one end of dowel in a pencil sharpener and
use it to score vein lines on calyx (E) and leaf cluster (F) as
shown in patterns.

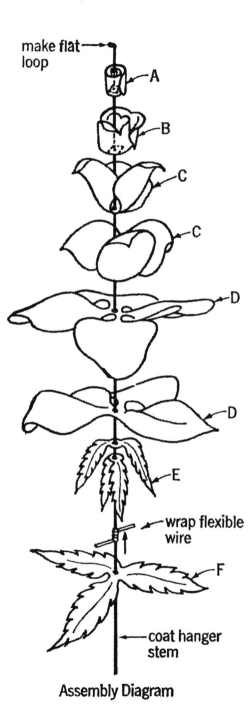

make flat loop

A

B

C

C

D

D

E

wrap flexible wire

F

coat hanger stem

Assembly Diagram

Apply a coat of primer to all aluminum pieces to conceal beverage name. Spray-paint all petals the basic rose color such as pink, red, yellow, or white; let dry. Spray-paint calyx and leaf cluster green; let dry. To shade rose petals, use a darker tone of the basic color. For example, shade a pink rose with dark pink or rose, a red rose with maroon or purple, a yellow rose with gold. The white rose can be shaded with either pink or yellow. To apply shading, spray centers of petals C and D a darker tone; then shade both sides. To shade center sections A and B, move spray along lower straight edge, fading out about halfway up; shade both sides.

Following the assembly diagram, complete the final shaping of petals. Bend both C petals into cups so they fit inside each other to form a six-petal shape. Turn both D petals down slightly as shown. Roll up B petal starting at end marked Y, then turn scalloped tips marked X outward, and finally bend tab with hole inward. Check that rolled B petal fits snugly in C and trim corners of tab, if necessary, so that it fits in C. Roll up A petal tightly, starting at Z, again checking that it fits inside B with tab bent in. Shape calyx as shown.

With wire cutters cut hook off hanger, straighten wire, and cut a 12"- to 14"-long piece for rose stem. Following diagram, form a small flat loop as shown, using long-nosed pliers. Assemble all rose petals A through D, plus calyx (E) pieces as shown. Check that they fit snugly together, then with a length of No. 20-gauge flexible wire wrapped tightly against calyx as shown, cut excess wire. Dab a quick-drying epoxy on wrapped wire for extra holding strength; let dry. Slip leaf cluster on stem and attach the same way. Brush stem and wrapped wire mounds with green enamel; let dry. To finish enameled roses, spray with satin-finish varnish.

CHRISTMAS ORNAMENTS AND DECORATIONS

Embroidered Felt Ornaments

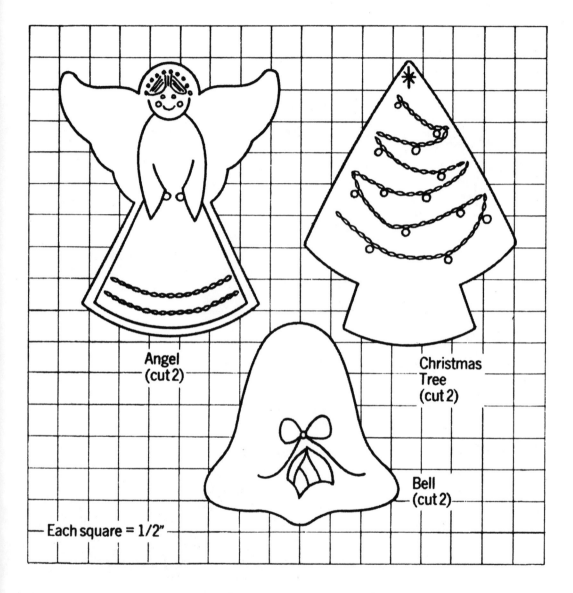

Angel
(cut 2)

Christmas
Tree
(cut 2)

Bell
(cut 2)

Each square = 1/2"

For Angel:
scraps white felt
light blue, pink, yellow, bright pink, and green 6-strand
    embroidery floss
white thread
gold metallic thread
absorbent cotton

For Christmas Tree:
scraps green felt
red 6-strand embroidery floss
gold metallic thread
absorbent cotton

For Bell:
scraps red felt
green and white 6-strand embroidery floss
gold metallic thread
absorbent cotton

Note: To enlarge patterns, see page 175.

Angel: Enlarge pattern on brown wrapping paper; cut out. Cut two angels from white felt, using pinking shears. Lightly pencil outline for dress, candle, and facial features on one felt angel. Using two strands of floss throughout, embroider hair,

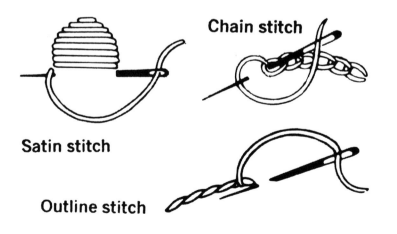

Satin stitch

Chain stitch

Outline stitch

eyes, cheeks, candle, and hands in satin stitch. Use an outline stitch to frame face, make mouth, and frame dress, sleeves, and collar. Use chain stitch to trim bottom edge of dress. Make a halo with metallic thread. Matching edges, sew angel together, outlining wings in blue, then continuing with white thread. Leave opening to stuff loosely with cotton; stuff, then close. For hanger loop use needle to thread length of gold thread through top edge; knot ends.

Christmas Tree: Enlarge pattern on brown wrapping paper; cut out. Cut two trees from green felt, using pinking shears. Lightly pencil guidelines for garland and ornament balls on one felt tree. Use a single strand of metallic thread to embroider garland in chain stitch and two strands of red floss to embroider balls in satin stitch. Make star at top as shown. Matching edges, sew tree together with red floss, leaving opening to stuff. Stuff lightly and close opening. Attach loop as described for angel.

Bell: Enlarge pattern on brown wrapping paper; cut out. Cut two bells from red felt, using pinking shears. Lightly pencil outline for bow and leaves on one felt bell. Use satin stitch for bow and outline stitch for leaves. Matching edges, sew bell together with green floss, leaving opening. Stuff lightly and close opening. Attach gold hanger loop as described for angel.

Cookie Ornaments

Each square = 1/2"

hole for hanger loop

Bird

Elephant

hole for hanger loop

Materials:
    see recipe below for special dough
    food coloring
    small candies, red hots, cake decorations such as silver balls,
        confetti, and florets
    florist's wire
    paring knife
    cardboard
    small artist's brushes
    clear polyurethane or shellac (optional)

Enlarge patterns for elephant and bird on cardboard according to directions on page 175; cut out.

Follow recipe below to make dough for cookies, which are inedible. Recipe cannot be halved or doubled. Cookies measure about 5", and recipe will make about 24.

Recipe: Preheat oven to 300°. Mix 4 cups flour with 1 cup salt. Dissolve ¼ cup instant coffee in 1½ cups warm water. Make a hole in center of flour-salt mixture and pour in 1 cup coffee. Mix thoroughly with hands or fork, adding additional coffee-water if necessary (dough should be smooth and satiny and neither crumbly nor sticky). Form into balls and store in plastic bags to prevent drying out. Using one ball at a time, roll out on cookie sheet to ¼" thickness. Use cardboard patterns to cut cookie shapes with wet paring knife. Pull away excess dough, knead into ball, and roll out again. To incise details on cookies, follow pattern and use tip of ice pick. Work a hole centered at top of each ornament and insert and twist a piece of wire for hanger. Following photograph, paint cookies with undiluted food coloring and artist's brushes. Press small candies and cake decorations into dough as shown.

Bake ornaments in 350° oven ¾ to 1½ hours or until pin inserted in dough comes out clean. Remove from oven and cool on cake rack. Coat with polyurethane or shellac if desired.

Crocheted Bells

SIZE: Each bell is about 3½" high.

MATERIALS:

Coats & Clark's Speed-Cro-Sheen, 1 (100-yard) ball each white, green, and red

aluminum crochet hook size F (or international size 4.00 mm), *or the size that will give you the correct gauge*

three 1"-diameter satin-ball ornaments

one 2½"-diameter wooden drapery ring

starch

GAUGE: 7 sc = 2"; 9 rnds = 2".

Using 2 strands crochet cotton, make one bell from each color as follows: Starting at center of top, ch 2. **1st rnd:** Work 8 sc in 2nd ch from hook; join with sl st in 1st sc. **2nd rnd:** Ch 1, 2 sc in same place as sl st, 2 sc in each sc (16 sc); join. **3rd rnd:** Ch 1, sc in same place as sl st, 2 sc in next sc, * sc in next sc, 2 sc in next sc. Repeat from * around (24 sc); join. **4th rnd:** Ch 1, sc in same place as sl st, sc in each sc; join. **5th rnd:** Ch 1, sc around, increasing 8 sc evenly spaced (32 sc); join. Repeat 4th rnd 10 times. Repeat 3rd and 4th rnds once (48 sc). **18th rnd:** Ch 1, sc in same place as sl st, sc in next sc, * 2 sc in next sc, sc in each of next 2 sc. Repeat from * around, ending 2 sc in last sc (64 sc); join; turn. **19th rnd:** Sl st in front lp of each sc on 18th rnd. Break off.

Following directions on box, make a medium-strength starch mixture. Saturate bell in mixture. Squeezing out excess, shape bell with hands, then stand it on pad of paper towels to dry.

Cut a length of crochet cotton and tie one end to satin ball (for clapper), then tie other end to inside of top of bell. Cut another length and tie one end to outside of top of bell for hanging cord.

With one strand green, work sc's over drapery ring until covered; sl st in 1st sc; break off.

Holding all three hanging cords together at desired lengths (see photograph), tie around covered ring.

Crocheted Snowmen

You can make a snowman small enough to hang from a tree limb or big enough to sit on the mantel. We give directions for both.

SIZES: Small snowman (tree ornament) is 4" tall; large snowman is 10½" tall.

MATERIALS:

For small snowman:

Coats & Clark's Speed-Cro-Sheen, small amounts each white, green, red, black, and orange

steel crochet hook No. 1, *or the size that will give you the correct gauge*

small amount Dacron polyester or cotton balls for stuffing

tapestry needle

For large snowman:

Coats & Clark's Speed-Cro-Sheen, 2 (100-yard) balls white, 1 ball green, and small amounts each red, black, and orange

steel crochet hook No. 00, *or the size that will give you the correct gauge*

Dacron polyester for stuffing

tapestry needle

Note: 2 balls white will make one small and one large snowman.

GAUGES: With No. 1 hook, 11 sc = 2"; 6 rnds = 1". With No. 00 hook, 9 sts = 2", 3 rnds h dc = 1".

To inc 1 st work 2 sts in same st.

To dec 1 sc draw up lp in each of next 2 sc, y o, and draw through all 3 lps on hook.

To dec 1 h dc (y o, draw up lp in next st) twice, y o, and draw through all 5 lps on hook.

SMALL SNOWMAN

BODY: Starting at bottom center with white, ch 2. **1st rnd:** Work 8 sc in 2nd ch from hook. Do not join rnds but mark beg of each rnd. **2nd rnd:** Work 2 sc in each sc (16 sc). **3rd rnd:** * Sc in next sc, 2 sc in next sc. Repeat from * around (24 sc). **4th rnd:** Sc in each sc, increasing 4 sc evenly spaced. **5th through 8th rnds:** Sc in each sc (28 sc). **9th through 12th rnds:** Sc in each sc, decreasing 3 sc, evenly spaced, on each rnd and being careful not to work decs directly above each other (16 sc); stuff. Continue to stuff as you work. **13th rnd:** Sc in each sc. **14th and 15th rnds:** Sc in each sc, increasing 3 sc evenly. **16th and 17th rnds:** Sc in each sc (22 sc). **18th and 19th rnds:** Sc in each sc, decreasing 3 sc evenly. **20th and 21st rnds:** * Draw up lp in each of next 2 sc, y

o, and draw through all 3 lps on hook. Repeat from * around. Break off.

Eyes and Buttons: Following photograph for placement, with black work a few straight stitches over a sc.

Nose: With orange sl st to a sc, ch 3, sl st in each ch. Break off.

SCARF: With red ch 34; sc in 2nd ch from hook and in each ch across. Break off. *For fringe* cut three 1½" lengths red and fold in half. Insert folded end through st at 1 end of scarf and pull ends through fold. Fray ends. Work another fringe at other end of scarf. Tie around snowman's neck.

HAT: Starting at top with green, ch 2. **1st rnd:** Work 6 sc in 2nd ch from hook. Do not join rnds but mark beg of rnds. **2nd rnd:** Work sc in each sc. **3rd rnd:** Sc in each sc, increasing 4 sc evenly. Repeat last 2 rnds once more, then repeat 2nd rnd once again. **7th rnd:** Work 2 sc in each sc (28 sc); sl st to 1st sc to join. Break off. Split an 8" length of green, thread one strand through top of hat, and tie ends together to form hanging loop. Tack hat to top of snowman.

LARGE SNOWMAN

BODY: Starting at center of underside with white, ch 3, join with sl st to form ring. **1st rnd:** Ch 2, work 8 h dc in ring (9 h dc, counting ch 2 as 1 h dc). Do not join rnds but mark beg of rnds. **2nd rnd:** Work 2 h dc in each h dc (18 h dc). **3rd rnd:** * H dc in next st, 2 h dc in next st. Repeat from * around (27 h dc). **4th through 10th rnds:** H dc in each st, increasing 7 h dc evenly spaced around. **11th through 16th rnds:** H dc in each h dc (76 h dc). **17th through 23rd rnds:** H dc in each st, decreasing 7 h dc evenly spaced around (27 h dc); stuff. Continue to stuff as you work. **24th through 27th rnds:** H dc in each st, increasing 5 h dc evenly spaced (47 h dc). **28th rnd:** H dc in each st, increasing 3 h dc. **29th through 31st rnds:** H dc in each st (50 h dc). **32nd through 36th rnds:** H dc in each st, decreasing 8 h dc evenly (10 h dc). **37th rnd:** * (Y o and draw up lp in next st) twice, y o, and draw through all lps on hook. Repeat from * around. Break off.

Eyes, Mouth, and Buttons: Following photograph, with black work as for small snowman.

Nose: With 2 strands orange sl st to a sc, ch 5, sl st in each ch. Break off.

SCARF: With red ch 91. **1st row:** Sc in 2nd ch from hook and in each ch across (90 sc); ch 1, turn. **2nd row:** Sc in each sc; ch 1, turn. Repeat last rnd once more, omitting ch 1. Break off. **Fringe:** Work 3 fringes along each end of scarf as for small snowman, cutting three 4″ lengths for each fringe.

HAT: Starting at top with green, ch 3. Join with sl st to form ring. **1st rnd:** Ch 1, work 5 sc in ring; sl st in ch 1 to join. **2nd rnd:** Ch 1, sc in each sc, increasing 2 sc evenly spaced; join. **3rd rnd:** Ch 1, sc in each sc, increasing 3 sc; join. **4th rnd:** Ch 1, sc in each sc, increasing 5 sc; join. **5th rnd:** Ch 1, sc in each sc, increasing 7 sc; join. **6th and 7th rnds:** Ch 1, sc in each sc (22 sc); join. **8th rnd:** Ch 1, sc in each sc, increasing 7 sc; join. **9th rnd:** Repeat 6th rnd (29 sc). **10th rnd:** Ch 1, sc in each sc, increasing 10 sc; join. **11th and 12th rnds:** Repeat 6th rnd. **13th rnd:** Repeat 10th rnd (49 sc). **14th through 16th rnds:** Repeat 6th rnd. **17th rnd:** Ch 1, work 2 sc in each sc (98 sc); join. **18th rnd:** Repeat 6th rnd. Break off. Tack to snowman's head.

Coffee Dough Wreath

Instant coffee gives a delicate tint to this utterly charming baked wreath of fruits and nuts (7"). It's a project children could spend absorbing hours over. Shellac provides the shine.

Follow recipe below to make dough wreath, which is inedible. Recipe, which will make several wreaths, cannot be halved or doubled.

Preheat oven to 300°F. Combine 4 cups unsifted all-purpose flour with 1 cup salt. Dissolve ¼ cup instant coffee in 1½ cups warm water. Make a hole in the center of the flour-salt mixture and pour in 1 cup coffee-water. Mix thoroughly with fork or hands, adding additional coffee-water if necessary. Dough should be smooth and satiny and neither crumbly nor sticky. Form into balls and place in plastic bags to prevent drying out. Use one ball at a time.

Working on aluminum foil, form a ¼"-thick 6"-diameter ring with a 3¼"-diameter centered hole, for base of wreath. Referring to photograph, make ¼"-thick x ½" x 1½" leaves, cutting out shapes with a wet knife. To keep wreath in scale, make larger fruit shapes first. Fill in with smaller fruit shapes and nuts. To attach dough pieces to ring, brush with water and press shapes in place. Texture leaves and fruit with sharp point of a pencil or knife.

Bake wreath on foil for an hour, or until hard. When cool, peel away foil and apply two coats of shellac, front and back, to preserve.

Birds-of-a-Feather Tree

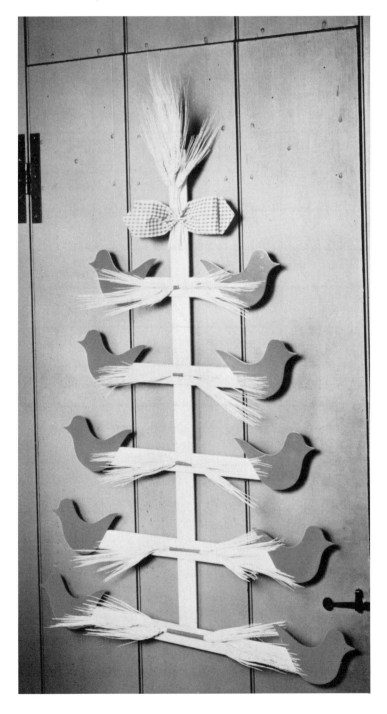

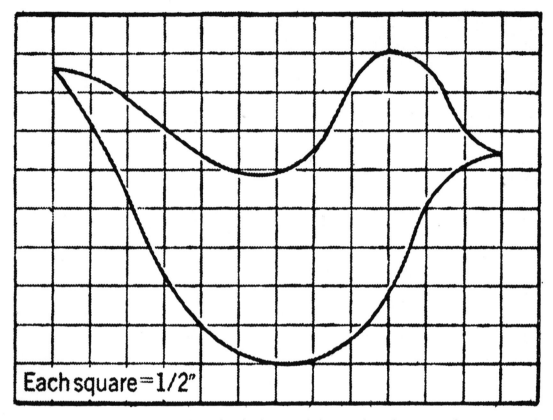

Each square = 1/2"

Fronds of wheat and the gingham bow give this tree a rustic look. The hardboard birds are painted with glossy red enamel.

Size: 30" tall.

Materials:
    9' length ¼" x 1¼" pine lattice
    18" x 24" piece ¼" hardboard
    3 bunches natural dried wheat
    2 skeins 6-strand red embroidery floss
    1 yard 2"-wide red and white gingham ribbon
    white glue
    fine flexible wire
    pigmented-shellac primer
    high-gloss red enamel

For tree, cut following pieces from lattice: 25" vertical strip and 22", 18", 14", 10", and 6" crosspieces. Following photograph, center and glue longest crosspiece across one end of vertical strip, then glue remaining crosspieces to strip in descending order 3" apart. Drill hole through top of vertical strip for hanging. Put aside.

Enlarge pattern for bird according to directions on page 175; cut out. Using pattern and jigsaw, cut 10 birds from hardboard. Sand cut edges. Apply primer to all birds; let dry. Spray-paint birds red; let dry. Glue birds on ends of crosspieces as shown.

Cut 6 to 8 pieces of wheat to make double sheaves as in photograph. Bind each sheaf in middle with embroidery floss; knot ends. Center and glue sheaves on crosspieces.

To finish, bind wheat sheaf for treetop with wire. Make flat 10"-wide bow as shown. Glue wheat and bow to treetop.

Sleepy Santa Pillow

Size: About 12″ in diameter.
Materials:

    36″-wide cotton fabrics, ½ yard polka-dot print, ⅜ yard
      each candy stripes and calico

    7″ x 16″ piece pink cotton

    scraps red cotton and bright pink felt

    ½ yard 36″-wide red felt for hat

    2 ounces white bulky yarn for beard

    small amounts red, green, and blue knitting worsted for
      pompon

    scrap dark blue 6-strand embroidery floss for eyes

    polyester for stuffing

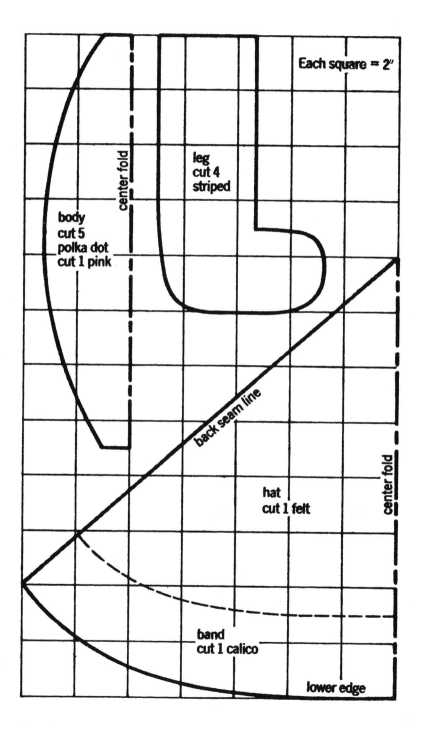

Each square = 2"

center fold

leg
cut 4
striped

body
cut 5
polka dot
cut 1 pink

back seam line

center fold

hat
cut 1 felt

band
cut 1 calico

lower edge

Patterns: Enlarge diagram according to directions on page 175, and cut paper patterns, adding ½" seam allowance to all edges.

Using patterns, cut fabric pieces.

Body: With right sides facing, stitch two body pieces together along one long side. Stitch third piece to second and so on until all body pieces are joined. Stitch remaining long edges of first and sixth pieces together so that unit forms deflated ball open at top and bottom. Cut calico circle to fit over one open end of ball. Turn under seam around circle and blindstitch over opening. Stuff body firmly. Cut another calico circle and sew over other opening.

Cut two 5" circles from red fabric. Stitch together, leaving opening for turning. Turn and stuff. Close opening. Sew to pink body panel for nose. Cut two 2¼" bright pink felt circles and sew on for cheeks. Using twelve strands floss, embroider eyes in outline stitch.

Following photograph for placement, lightly mark with pins or chalk three lines about 1" apart for beard. Tack end of bulky yarn to one end of lowest line. Make 1½"-long loops across line, tacking them as you go. Make loops across remaining two lines.

Legs: With right sides facing, stitch pairs of leg pieces together, leaving tops open. Turn and stuff softly with very little stuffing at top. Turn under seams at top and pinch flat with leg seams at center front and back. Sew legs to bottom of body so that Santa will sit up.

Hat: With right side of calico band against felt hat, stitch around lower edge. Trim seam and turn band to right side. Turn under seam along opposite edge of band and topstitch to hat. Fold hat in half, wrong side out, and stitch back seam. Turn.

Make 2½"-diameter pompon with red, green, and blue yarn and tie to top of hat.

TOYS
AND OTHER
KID STUFF

Clown Head Crib Toys

These laughing clowns have 4" knitted heads, filled with nylon net. The muffled bell is deep inside where baby can't reach it.

SIZE: 4" in diameter.

MATERIALS:

   orlon acrylic knitting worsted, one ounce of blue or red (color A) for clown's face, small amounts hot pink (B), white (C), orange (D), and olive (E) for round head, or blue green (F), yellow (G), and light blue (H) for pointed head

   a few yards each of light blue and red yarn or black and white yarn for features

   knitting needles, 1 set (4) double-pointed No. 3 (or English needles No. 10), *or the size that will give you the correct gauge*

   tapestry needle

   nylon net for stuffing (this material is lightweight and washable)

   1 bell for each head

GAUGE: 5 sts = 1".

NOTE: Cut net into strips and stuff head as you work. Also insert bell.

ROUND HEAD

Starting at bottom with A, cast on 9 sts. Divide sts evenly on 3 needles and join, being careful not to twist sts. **1st rnd:** K around, increasing 1 st in each st (18 sts). **2nd rnd:** K around. **3rd rnd:** (K 1, inc in next st) 9 times (27 sts). K 2 rnds even. **6th rnd:** (K 2, inc in next st) 9 times (36 sts). K 2 rnds even. **9th rnd:** (K 3, inc in next st) 9 times (45 sts). K 2 rnds even. **12th rnd:** (K 4, inc in next st) 9 times (54 sts). K 2 rnds even. **15th rnd:** (K 5, inc in next st) 9 times (63 sts). K 2 rnds even. **18th rnd:** (K 6, inc in next st) 9 times (72 sts). K 2 rnds even. **21st rnd:** (K 6, k 2 tog) 9 times (63 sts). K 2 rnds even. **24th rnd:** (K 5, k 2 tog) 9 times (54 sts).

Break off A; attach B and k 1 rnd. **26th rnd:** (K 4, k 2 tog) 9 times (45 sts). Break off B; attach C and k 1 rnd. Break off C; attach D and k 1 rnd. **29th rnd:** (K 3, k 2 tog) 9 times (36 sts). Break off D; attach C and k 1 rnd. Break off C; attach B and k 1 rnd. **32nd rnd:** (K 2, k 2 tog) 9 times (27 sts). Break off B; attach C and k 1 rnd. Break off C; attach D and k 1 rnd. **35th rnd:** (K 1, k 2 tog) 9 times (18 sts). Break off D; attach C and k 1 rnd.

Break off C; attach B and k 1 rnd. **38th rnd:** K 2 tog around (9 sts). K 1 rnd. Break off, leaving 6″ end. Thread in tapestry needle, draw through sts. Pull up and fasten.

Pompon: Stuff with bits of yarn as you work. With D, work as for head through 3rd rnd (27 sts). K 1 rnd even. **5th rnd:** (K 1, k 2 tog) 9 times (18 sts). K 1 rnd even. **7th rnd:** K 2 tog around (9 sts). K 1 rnd even. Finish as for head. Sew to top of head.

Nose: With D, work as for head through 3rd rnd. K 2 rnds even. Bind off. Stuff with yarn and sew to face.

Ears: With E, cast on 11 sts and work with 2 needles. K 1 row, p 1 row. **3rd row:** K 1, sl 1, k 1, psso, k 5, k 2 tog, k 1. **4th row and every even-numbered row:** P across. **5th row:** K 1, sl 1, k 1, psso, k 3, k 2 tog, k 1. **7th row:** K 1, sl 1, k 1, psso, k 1, k 2 tog, k 1. **9th row:** K 1, (inc in next st, k 1) twice. **11th row:** K 1, inc in next st, k 3, inc in next st, k 1. **13th row:** K 1, inc in next st, k 5, inc in next st, k 1 (11 sts). Bind off. Sew sides to form cup. Stuff with yarn and sew to side of head. Make other ear in same manner.

Following photograph for placement, em-broider light blue eyes and red mouth in chain st.

POINTED HEAD

Work as for round head through 18th rnd. K 5 rnds even. **24th rnd:** (K 6, k 2 tog) 9 times (63 sts). Break off A; attach F and k 4 rnds. **29th rnd:** (K 5, k 2 tog) 9 times (54 sts). Break off F; attach G and k 2 rnds. Break off G; attach H and k 3 rnds. **35th rnd:** (K 4, k 2 tog) 9 times (45 sts). Break off H; attach G and k 2 rnds. Break off G; attach F and k 3 rnds. **41st rnd:** (K 3, k 2 tog) 9 times (36 sts). Break off F; attach G and k 2 rnds. Break off G; attach H and k 3 rnds. **47th rnd:** (K 2, k 2 tog) 9 times (27 sts). Break off H; attach G and k 2 rnds. Break off G; attach F and k 3 rnds. **53rd rnd:** (K 1, k 2 tog) 9 times (18 sts). Break off F; attach G and k 2 rnds. Break off G; attach H and k 3 rnds. **59th rnd:** K 2 tog around (9 sts). Finish and fasten off as for round head.

Make pompon with A, nose with G, and ears with H, following directions for round head. Following photograph for placement, em-broider black eyes and white mouth in chain st.

Pig and Beanbag Piglets

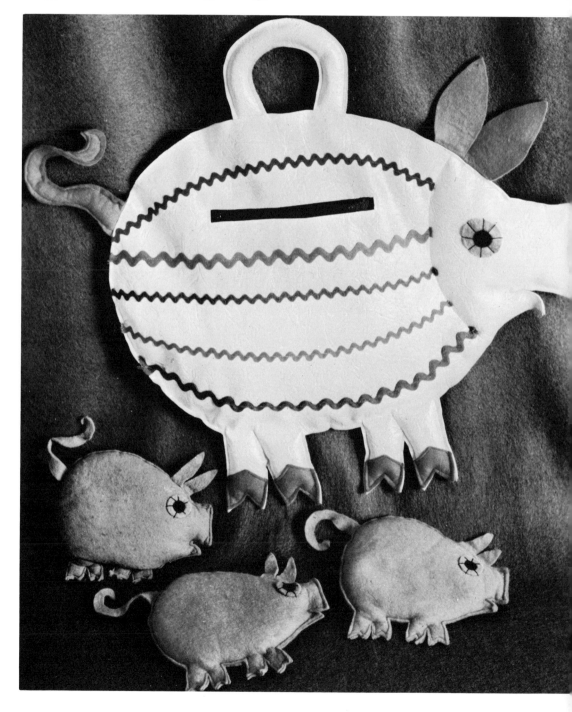

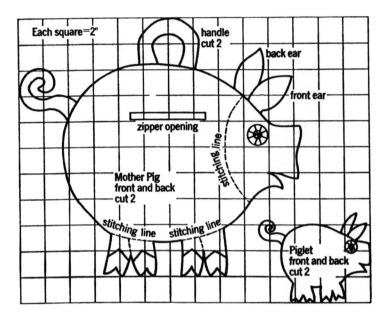

Mother pig has a tummyful of beanbag piglets. She's vinyl trimmed with rickrack and felt, 18½″ long. The piglets are all felt. Mama can hold five or more piglets.

Materials:
    ½ yard 54″-wide vinyl
    small amounts of cotton batting or nylon stockings cut in strips for stuffing
    five scrap lengths assorted colors and widths rickrack trim
    7″ skirt zipper
    felt scraps to trim pigs
    16″ x 16″ piece felt or cotton-print fabric for each piglet
    dry beans or rice
    matching thread

Mother Pig: Enlarge patterns according to directions on page 175 for body, handle, tail, ears, and hooves. Using patterns, cut body and handle from vinyl, adding ½″ seam allowance to ends of handle pieces only. Cut one each front and back ears, two tail pieces, and four hooves from scrap felt, adding seam allowance to end of ears and tail to be inserted into body. Referring to body pattern, cut opening for zipper and insert, following manufacturer's directions. Topstitch rickrack to body as in photograph. Topstitch felt hooves to feet. For eye cut two felt circles as in pattern and, using an overcast stitch, attach as shown. With right sides out, topstitch tail and handle pieces, leaving lower edge open. Stuff both loosely. Following photograph for placement, pin tail, handle, and ears to wrong side of pig front. Matching raw edges, topstitch pig back and front together with tail, handle, and ears sandwiched between. Leave opening by legs and head; stuff legs and head within stitching lines as indicated. Close openings and topstitch lines for head and legs.

Piglets: Enlarge pattern for piglet on brown wrapping paper. Cut two body pieces and one tail piece from felt for each piglet and do *not* add seam allowance. If making fabric piglets, allow ½" for seams all around and cut one felt tail piece. For all piglets, following pattern, cut two pieces of felt for eye and attach as described for mother pig. For felt piglets, matching edges, insert felt tail as in photograph and topstitch all around, leaving 2" opening for filling. For fabric piglets, pin body with right sides together; stitch, leaving opening to turn at tail area. Turn, fill piglets with beans or rice. Insert tail and close opening.

Three Wooden Toys

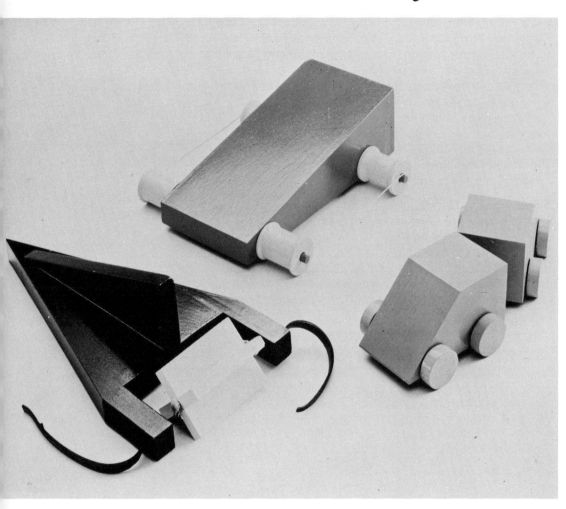

Wooden toys of simple design give children's imagination free rein.

For boat:
1' length 1 x 8 clear pine stock
two 2" heavy-duty rubber bands
small tacks
scrap ¼"-diameter dowel

For car:
2' length 1 x 4 clear pine stock
1' length ¼"-diameter dowel
No. 18-gauge wire
four wooden spools, all the same size

For train:
6" piece 2 x 2 pine stock
scrap 1"-diameter dowel
string
eight washers
1' length ¼"-diameter dowel

For all toys:
pigmented-shellac primer
waterproof glue
glossy enamels

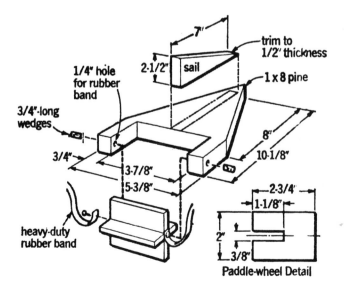

Paddle-wheel Detail

For Boat: Using diagram, mark and cut from 1 x 8 pine body for boat, triangular piece for sail and one paddle piece. Trim sail to ½" thickness and slice paddle piece into two approximately ¼"-thick pieces. Following paddle detail, notch paddle pieces. Mark and drill ¼"-diameter holes as indicated. Sand all boat pieces smooth. Assemble as in diagram. Prime and paint boat and paddle wheel as in photograph. To assemble paddle wheel between extensions at stern, cut rubber bands in 4" pieces and tack to paddle wheel, embedding tack head in rubber band. Thread loose band ends through ¼" holes in boat extensions; cut tiny wedges from ¼" dowel and insert to hold bands in place as shown.

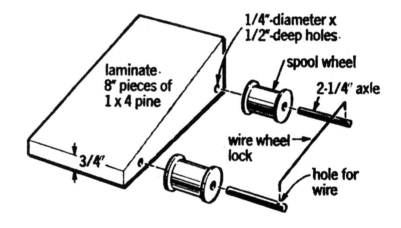

For Car: Mark and cut 1 x 4 pine into three 8" pieces; laminate pieces together for solid block. Following diagram, mark block for angled slope cut. Mark and drill ½"-deep holes for ¼" dowel on sides of car as shown. Cut dowel in four 2¼" pieces and drill a hole to fit wire wheel locks through dowel approximately ¹⁄₁₆" from end. Cut and bend wire as shown. Glue dowels in car for wheel posts. Sand car smooth, breaking all sharp edges. Prime and paint car and spools as in photograph. Assemble spool wheels on wheel posts, using wheel locks. Bend ends of wire against dowel.

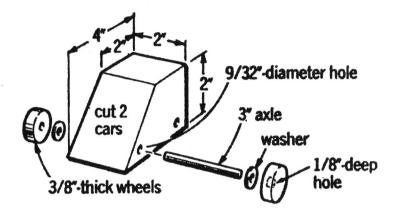

For Train: Mark for angled slope, as shown in diagram, on side of 2 x 2 pine; cut two train cars. Slice 1" dowel for wheels in eight ⅜"-thick pieces. Cut four 3" pieces of ¼" dowel for axles. Mark and drill ¼"-diameter holes through train cars and centered through wheels for axles as shown. Sand all train pieces smooth. Prime and paint pieces. Assemble train as shown. To hook cars together, staple a small loop of string to bottom of one car and a short piece of string with large knotted end to bottom of other car. Slip knot through loop.

SIZE: About 13½" tall.

MATERIALS:

    synthetic knitting-worsted-weight yarn, 1 ounce each turquoise (color A), orange (B), red (C), and 2 ounces yellow (D)

    aluminum crochet hook size H (or Canadian hook No. 8), *or the size that will give you the correct gauge*

    1½ yards cotton cord

    tapestry needle

    thin cardboard

GAUGE: Small disks measure about 1½" in diameter; large disks, about 2½" in diameter.

SMALL DISKS (make 1 each of A, B, C, and D): Starting at center, ch 4; join with sl st to form ring. **1st rnd:** Ch 3, work 11 dc in ring (12 dc, counting ch-3 as 1 dc); join with sl st to top of ch-3. Break off.

LARGE DISKS (make 25 A and 10 each of B, C, and D): Work as for small disk through first rnd; do not break off. **2nd rnd:** Ch 3, dc in same place as last sl st made, work 2 dc in each dc around (24 dc); join. Break off.

POMPON HEAD: From cardboard cut two disks 3" in diameter. Cut 1" hole in center of each disk. Make a slit in each cardboard disk from outer edge to hole. Hold disks together with slits matching. Working with two strands of D, wind yarn around disks by drawing it through slit to center and around outer edge. When disks are completely covered and center is filled, slip scissors between disks and cut yarn along outside edge. Separate disks slightly and wind a strand of yarn around center of yarn between disks; knot securely; break off. Remove disks; fluff pompon and trim.

HANDS AND FEET: Cut two cardboard disks 1½" in diameter. Cut ½" center holes. Make four pompons as for head.

ASSEMBLING: Thread a 36" length of cord; tie knot at end. Pull needle through center of pompon head, then thread small disks A, B, C, and D for neck, fifteen large A disks for body, one large disk each D, C, B, and A three times for leg, then small pompon for foot. Pull cord back through foot and leg into center of last body disk; make another leg and foot; rerun cord back through foot, leg, body, neck, and head; knot securely. Break off.

    Thread an 18" length of cord; tie knot at end. Secure cord to body cord below fifth body disk from neck, thread one large disk each D, C, B, and A twice for arm, then pompon for hand. Pull cord back to body cord; fasten. Work other arm and hand; rerun cord back to body; knot securely. Break off.

Fish Pillow

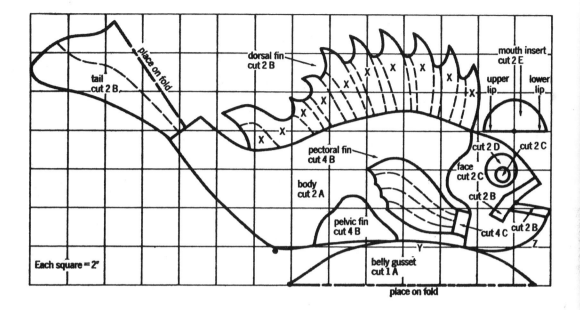

Each square = 2"

dorsal fin cut 2 B

tail cut 2 B

place on fold

mouth insert cut 2 E

upper lip   lower lip

cut 2 D   cut 2 C

face cut 2 C

cut 2 B

pectoral fin cut 4 B

body cut 2 A

pelvic fin cut 4 B

cut 4 C   cut 2 B

belly gusset cut 1 A

place on fold

Size: About 27" long.

Materials:

½ yard each 45"-wide red, white, and blue cotton print (A) and red polka-dot cotton (B)

small amount turquoise polka-dot cotton (C)

scraps red calico (D) and pink polka-dot cotton (E)

polyester for stuffing

black felt-tip pen

Enlarge diagram according to instructions on page 175 and cut pattern pieces, adding ¼" seam allowance to lips, eyes, and jagged edges of dorsal and pectoral fins and ½" seams to all other edges. Cut out fabric pieces indicated on patterns.

First Side: Press under raw edges of one C and one D eye section; topstitch to face. Turn under outer edges of lips; topstitch to face. With right sides together, matching raw edges and dots, seam mouth insert to lips (excess fabric of mouth insert will be pushed inside fish later).

Pectoral Fin: With right sides facing, stitch one C and one B fin piece together. Repeat for underside of same fin. With right sides together, stitch fin sections, leaving C end open. Trim seams and clip curves; turn. Stuff; topstitch along broken lines.

With right sides facing and pectoral fin sandwiched in position, stitch face and body sections together, catching fin in the stitching.

Seam two pelvic fin pieces together, leaving belly edge open; trim seam and clip curves; turn.

Second Side: Work same as for first side.

Dorsal Fin: With right sides facing, stitch fin pieces together, leaving body edge open; trim seam and clip curves; turn. Topstitch along broken lines. Stuff sections marked X.

Tail: Seam tail pieces together, leaving narrow end opening. Trim seam and clip curves; turn. Stuff. Topstitch along broken lines.

Assembly: With right sides facing, pin upper edges of fish together, with dorsal fin and tail sandwiched in position between sections. (*Note:* Fold wide end of tail in half and pin with safety pin to body of fish so it will not catch in stitching.) With right sides facing, matching dots, pin gusset between fish sides, with pelvic fins sandwiched in position. Starting at Y on diagram, stitch along gusset, lower edge of body, across base of tail, along upper edge of body, around face to Z on diagram, leaving opening from Y to Z. Stitch other side of gusset to body. Trim seams and clip curves; turn. Remove safety pin. Stuff body; blindstitch opening closed. Push mouth insert to inside. Draw pupil in center of eye with marker.

Cuddly Crocheted Lambs

SIZES: Papa Sheep: about 18" long. *Mama Sheep:* about 16" long. *Baby Lamb:* about 12" long.
MATERIALS:

For Papa:

Stanley Berroco (see Yarn Source, below) "Sportene" (loopy wool/viscose yarn), 5 (2-ounce) skeins Gray Mix No. 5-460-525 (color A)

For Mama:

Stanley Berroco "Featherloop" (loopy wool/nylon yarn), 4 (2-ounce) skeins Natural No. 5-777-100 (color B)

For Baby:

2 (2-ounce) skeins "Sportene" Gray Mix No. 5-460-525 (color A) and 1 (2-ounce) skein "Featherloop" Natural No. 5-777-100 (color B).

For each sheep you will also need a small amount black yarn in knitting-worsted weight

aluminum crochet hook size H (or Canadian hook No. 8), *or the size that will give you the correct gauge*

scraps black and white felt for eyes and nose

polyester stuffing

tapestry needle

ribbon for neck trimming, if desired

YARN SOURCE: If you have difficulty obtaining the yarn specified for these sheep, you can write to the following address for mail orders: Stanley Berroco, Inc., Dept. WD-2, 140 Mendon Street, Uxbridge, Massachusetts 01569.

GAUGE: 3 sts = 1", using yarn double.

Note: Use yarn held double throughout except when using black yarn for hooves.

PAPA SHEEP

Note: If you are making more than one animal, label small sections as you work to simplify assembly. Loops are added later.

BODY: Starting at tail end with 2 strands A, ch 2. **1st rnd:** Work 6 sc in 2nd ch from hook. Do not join, but work around in spiral fashion and mark beg of rnds. **2nd rnd:** Work 2 sc in each sc around. **3rd rnd:** Sc in each sc around, increasing 6 sc evenly spaced. Repeat last rnd 5 times more (48 sc), being careful not to work increases directly over those on previous rnd. **Next rnd:** Sc in each sc around, increasing 3 sc evenly spaced

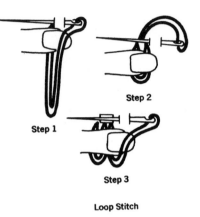

Step 1

Step 2

Step 3

Loop Stitch

(51 sc). Sc in each sc around until body measures 10½" from beg.

Stuff body firmly, then dec as follows and continue to stuff as needed. **Next rnd:** * Sc in next 15 sc; draw up lp in each of next 2 sc, y o, and draw through all 3 lps on hook (1 sc dec). Repeat from * around (48 sc). Continue working sc in each sc around, decreasing 6 sts evenly spaced (do not work decreases directly over those on previous rnds) until 6 sc remain. Dec 4 sc on next rnd. Break off, leaving 6" end. Add more stuffing if necessary, then sew opening closed.

HEAD (make 2 pieces): Work as for body through 6th rnd (36 sc). **Next rnd:** Sc in each sc around, increasing 4 sc evenly spaced (40 sc). Work 2 rnds even. Join with sl st in next sc and break off. Piece should measure about 6" in diameter when stretched.

EAR (make 2): Starting at one narrow end with 2 strands A, ch 2. **1st row:** Work 4 sc in 2nd ch from hook; ch 1, turn. **2nd row:** Work 2 sc in 1st sc, sc in each of next 2 sc, work 2 sc in last sc; ch 1, turn. Work even on 6 sc until ear measures 3". Dec 1 sc at beg and end of next 2 rows. Break off.

SNOUT: Work as for body through 4th rnd (24 sc). Work even for 1 rnd. Join and break off.

HOOF AND LEG (make 4): With 1 strand black ch 2. **1st rnd:** Work 8 sc in 2nd ch from hook. **2nd rnd (inc rnd):** Work 2 sc in 1st sc, sc in next sc, work 2 sc in each of next 3 sc, sc in next sc, work 2 sc in each of next 2 sc (14 sc). **3rd rnd:** Inc 3 sc evenly around (17 sc). **4th rnd (dec rnd):** Working in back lp only of each st, (draw up lp in each of next 2 sc, y o and draw through all 3 lps on hook, sc in next sc) 5 times; sl st in each of next 2 sc. Join with sl st in 1st sc of this rnd; break off. There are 12 sts on last rnd; hoof is completed.

For Leg: With 2 strands A work sc in each st around for 1 rnd (12 sc). Stuff hoof with a bit of black yarn, then continue to work even with 2 strands A until leg section measures 4" from beg. Sl st in next sc and break off.

TAIL (make 2 pieces): Starting at tip with 2 strands A, ch 2. **1st row:** Work 4 sc in 2nd ch from hook; ch 1, turn. **2nd and 3rd rows:** Work 2 sc in 1st sc, sc in each sc to within last sc, 2 sc in last sc; ch 1, turn. Work even on 8 sc until tail measures 3" from beg. Dec 1 st at beg and end of next row, then work even on 6 sc for 1 row. Break off.

TOPKNOT: With 2 strands A ch 2. **1st rnd:** Work 8 sc in 2nd ch from hook. Working sc in each sc, inc 8 sc evenly on each of next 3 rnds (32 sc). Work even for 1 rnd. Join and break off.

LOOPS: Thread 1 strand A into tapestry needle and, following directions for loop st, below, and diagrams, work loops on one side of topknot, top half of each leg and tail, along back half of head, and over most of body except for underside near back.

To Make Loops: Use 1 strand yarn. Make each loop about ¾" long. **Step 1:** Draw yarn to right side of work; with left thumb hold yarn down, skip ¼" of crochet to right and insert needle from right to left, bringing needle up in front of place where yarn emerges from crochet. Using thumb as a gauge for ¾" loop, draw yarn through to form loop over thumb. **Step 2:** Remove thumb from loop and hold loop down and yarn up as shown on diagram. Skip ¼" of crochet to right and insert needle from right to left, bringing needle up in front of last stitch. Draw yarn tight to fasten stitch. **Step 3:** Hold yarn down as in Step 1 and make loop as in Step 1. Then make stitch to fasten as in Step 2. Continue to work loops as specified.

FINISHING: Sew head pieces together, leaving opening for stuffing. Stuff; sew opening closed. Sew head to body. Sew snout, following photograph for position and stuffing lightly. Making a pleat at lower edge of each ear, sew lower edge to head. Sew topknot on head between ears.

Eyes and Nose: Cut ¾"-long oval pieces from black and white felt. Cut small triangle for nose from black felt. Sew eyes and nose in place. Use a few strands black yarn for eyelashes.

Stuff legs and sew to body. Pinch together front edge of hooves. Sew tail pieces together, leaving straight edge open. Stuff lightly; sew opening closed. Sew tail in place. Tie ribbon around neck.

MAMA SHEEP

Note: Work with 2 strands B held together throughout for all sections except when black yarn is used for hooves.

BODY: Work as for body of Papa Sheep.

HEAD (make 2 pieces): Work as for body of Papa Sheep through 6th rnd (36 sc). **Next rnd:** Sc in each sc around, increasing 4 sc evenly spaced (40 sc). Work 2 rnds even. Join with sl st in next sc and break off. Piece should measure about 6" when stretched.

EAR (make 2): Work as for ear of Papa Sheep.

SNOUT: Work as for body of Papa Sheep through 3rd rnd (18 sc). Work even for 1 rnd. Join; break off.

HOOF AND LEG (make 4): Work as for hoof of Papa Sheep, then work until leg section measures 3½" from beg. Sl st in next sc and break off.

TAIL: Work as for tail of Papa Sheep.

TOPKNOT: Work as for topknot of Papa Sheep.

FINISHING: Work as for Papa Sheep, but work loops on topknot only.

BABY LAMB

Note: Work with 1 strand each A and B held together throughout for all sections except when black yarn is used for hooves.

BODY: Work as for body of Papa Sheep through 4th rnd (24 sc). Work even in sc for 1 rnd. On next rnd inc 6 sc evenly spaced around. Work even in sc for 1 rnd. On next rnd inc 3 sc evenly spaced around (33 sc). Sc in each sc around until body measures 7½" from beg. Stuff body, then dec as follows, and stuff as needed.

Dec 3 sc evenly on next rnd, then work 1 rnd even. Dec 6 sc evenly on next rnd, then work 1 rnd even. Dec 6 sc evenly around on each rnd until 6 sc remain. Dec 4 sc on next rnd. Break off. Add more stuffing if necessary, then sew opening closed.

HEAD (make 2 pieces): Work as for body of Papa Sheep through 5th rnd (30 sc). Work even for 1 rnd. Join and break off. Piece should measure about 4½" in diameter when stretched.

EAR (make 2): Ch 2. **1st row:** Work 3 sc in 2nd ch from hook; ch 1, turn. **2nd row:** Inc 1 sc in 1st sc, sc in next sc, inc 1 sc in last sc; ch 1, turn. Work even on 5 sc until ear measures 2½" from beg. Dec 1 sc at beg and end of next 2 rows. Break off.

SNOUT: Ch 2. **1st rnd:** Work 5 sc in 2nd sc. **2nd rnd:** Work 2 sc in each sc. **3rd rnd:** Inc 5 sc evenly around. **4th rnd:** Sc in each sc around (15 sc). Join and break off.

HOOF AND LEG (make 4): Work as for hoof and leg of Papa Sheep through 2nd rnd (14 sc). **3rd rnd (dec rnd):** Working in back lp only (draw up lp in each of next 2 sc, y o and draw through all lps on hook, sc in next sc) 4 times; sl st in each of next 2 sc. Join with sl st in 1st sc. Break off. There are 10 sts on last rnd; hoof is completed.

For Leg: With A and B, sc in each st around (10 sc). Stuff hoof with a bit of black yarn, then continue to work even with A and B until leg section measures 3" from beg. Sl st in next sc and break off.

TAIL (make 2 pieces): Work as for tail of Papa Sheep through 2nd rnd. Work even on 6 sc until tail measures 2" from beg. Dec 1 st at beg and end of next row. Break off.

TOPKNOT: Ch 2. **1st rnd:** Work 8 sc in 2nd ch from hook. Working sc in each sc, inc 8 sc evenly spaced on each of next 2 rnds (24 sc). Work 1 rnd even. Join and break off.

FINISHING: Work as for Papa Sheep, making eyes ½" ovals and working loops on topknot only.

Pocket-Size Dollmates

112

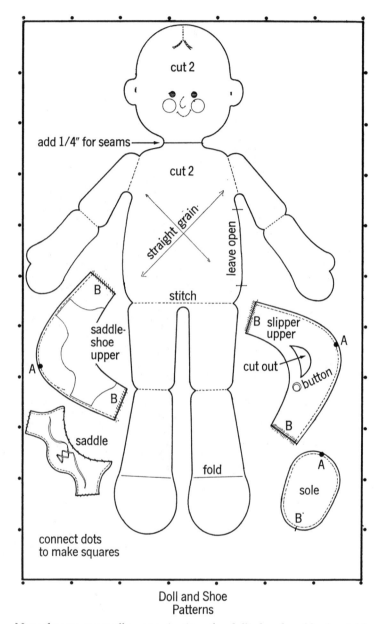

cut 2

add 1/4" for seams

cut 2

straight grain

leave open

stitch

B

saddle-
shoe
upper

A

B

saddle

B slipper
upper

A

cut out

button

B

A

sole

B

fold

connect dots
to make squares

Doll and Shoe
Patterns

Note that no seam allowance is given for doll's head and body. Add
¼" to pattern.

Little girls love little things. They also love look-alikes. So what
better way to fulfill a moppet's dream than with this small
stuffed doll designed for you to make ad infinitum. Cut out
several at once. Finish one in an evening. Just 8½" from head to
toe, our charming doll has an articulated body, can be walked,
skipped, somersaulted into a child's make-believe world. Vary
the body fabric color for a one-world family of dolls or do a doll
duplicate of your own child or some of her friends, using
leftover fabrics from their dresses.

The four dolls, their panties, and dresses are all made from
identical patterns. See photograph for colors and details.

GENERAL DIRECTIONS

To enlarge patterns, make a grid of squares with colored pencil
by connecting dots across patterns from one side to opposite
side. Then, with ruler and triangle, draw a grid of 1" squares on
a piece of paper, making the same number of squares as on
pattern. Copy in each square the same lines you see in corresponding pattern square.

Cut out enlarged patterns along outer edges, which include
¼" seam allowance on doll, except for joining of head to body
at neck; add ¼" to neck edges. Panties and dresses have ⅛"
seam allowance.

Pin patterns on fabric and cut out. If two identical pieces are
to be cut from fabric with a right and wrong side, reverse
pattern to cut second piece. Trace very small or narrow patterns on fabric, stitch first, then cut out.

DOLL

Materials for one:
  percale, ¼ yard 42" wide or piece 9" x 18" in light pink,
    peach, or brown
  matching thread
  black floss
  Dacron polyester, kapok, or cotton stuffing
  1-ounce skein knitting worsted or sports yarn in brown,
    rust, black, or yellow

Cutting: Place patterns on percale on the bias and cut two body
and two head pieces, adding ¼" seam allowances at neck.

Sewing and Stuffing: Use fine machine stitching when possible, stitching twice so that ¼" seams can be trimmed close.

For head, seam front to back with right sides facing, leaving neck end open. Trim seams and turn; stuff firmly. Sew one stitch through each ear.

For face, lightly mark features with pencil. Using one strand of floss, satin-stitch eyes and outline-stitch nose and mouth. Rouge cheeks lightly with crayon.

For body, join front to back with ¼" seam, leaving opening at side and neck. Trim seams and turn.

Stuff feet and lower legs. Following Diagram 1, bend feet at 90° angle, fold in fabric at ankles, and sew. Stitch across legs for knees; add stuffing and stitch for hip joints; stuff body and arms. Sew side opening; stitch arm joints.

To assemble doll, pin head to body. Following Diagram 2, turn in seam allowances and sew, adding stuffing if necessary.

Hair: For long, braided hair, mark center part on head. Cut brown, rust, or yellow yarn into 22" lengths; thread through a needle, making a double 11" length. Beginning at face edge, take a stitch below ear, leaving 3½" ends for braid. Take a stitch under center part, then another below other ear, leaving 3½"

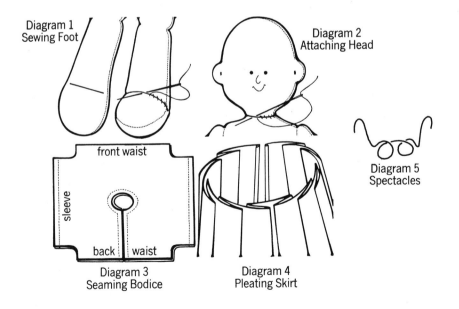

Diagram 1
Sewing Foot

Diagram 2
Attaching Head

Diagram 5
Spectacles

front waist

sleeve

back | waist

Diagram 3
Seaming Bodice

Diagram 4
Pleating Skirt

loop; clip open and remove needle. Repeat until head is completely covered. Make two thick braids and tie with yarn. Ravel braid ends. To emphasize part, backstitch or outline stitch over it with thread matching skin.

For Afro hairdo, cover head with loops of yarn, then clip loops, as follows: Thread black yarn in needle and double it. Take small stitch through head, leaving ¾" ends. Secure with a second tiny stitch almost in the same place. Make another stitch next to last, leaving ¾" loop. Secure with tiny stitch. Repeat to cover head thickly with yarn ends and loops; and clip to about ½" length.

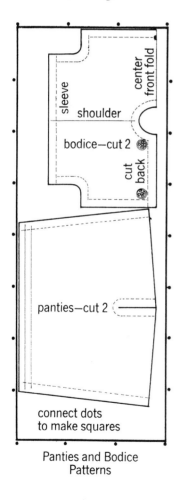

Panties and Bodice
Patterns

CLOTHES

Panties:

Material for one pair:
3" x 9" piece white cotton fabric
7" scrap each narrow lace and cord elastic

Pin pattern to fabric and cut two pieces, but do not cut crotch. Stitch crotch seam, then cut open. Seam sides. Hem legs and stitch casing at waist. Insert elastic, knot ends to fit, and trim. Turn panties and trim legs with lace.

Dresses:

Materials for a one-fabric dress:
8" x 16" piece printed cotton

For two-fabric dress:
4" x 15" print strip for skirt and 4" x 9" white piece for bodice

For each dress:
matching thread
2 snaps
9" scrap lace and pearl button for red and green print dress
three red beads for buttons on two-fabric dress

Bodice: (*Note:* Bodice is lined with self fabric.) Fold fabric and place bodice center of pattern on fold; cut out and slash back open; repeat for bodice lining. Unfold pieces and hold with right sides facing as in Diagram 3. Seam back opening, neckline, and sleeve ends only (for lace trim, insert it between bodice and lining, with right sides together and straight edges flush; then seam sleeve ends). Trim seams and turn. Seam sides and sleeves.

Skirt: Cut 3½" x 14¾" fabric strip. Stitch ⅛" hems on 3½" edges for back opening and ½" hem on one long edge. Mark center front of skirt. Following Diagram 4, mark, fold, and pin ten pleats at waistline edge to measure same as waist edge of bodice, with inverted box pleat at center. Press pleats and work two rows of machine stitching over them around top.

Assembly: With right sides together, pin skirt to bodice, making it desired length. Seam at waistline. Trim seam allowance, press up, and whip-stitch raw edge. Sew snaps to back neck and waist.

Shoes:

Materials for pair of strap slippers:
3″ x 5″ piece felt in either black, blue, or red for uppers
2″ x 4″ tan felt for soles

For saddle shoes:
3¼″ x 4½″ white felt
2½″ x 4″ brown felt and 2″ x 4″ tan felt for soles.
buttons or beads for slippers or white floss for shoelaces

Note: All upper and sole patterns are for right foot; reverse for left.

Slippers: Following two patterns, cut uppers and soles from felt. Mark center toes at A and center backs at B. Seam together backs of uppers with B edges just meeting, using a machine zigzag or hand overcast stitch (shown on pattern). Baste each upper to sole, matching A's and B's; machine-stitch or hand backstitch around dotted lines. Sew on buttons.

Saddle Shoes: Following three patterns, cut white uppers, brown saddles, and tan soles. Machine-stitch saddles along dotted lines to uppers; hand-sew at instep and sole edges (shown on pattern). Using three strands of floss for laces, make cross-stitches and tie ends in bows. Seam back edges of uppers and stitch to soles, following slipper directions.

Spectacles: See doll in blue print dress in color photograph and Diagram 5 to shape 5½″ length 24-gauge copper wire into spectacles frame.

About 1¼″ from one end, bend wire around a lead pencil to shape about ⅜″-diameter circle for an imaginary left lens. Leave ⅛″ for bridge and shape second circle to fit around doll's right eye. Curve ends to go over ears and trim if necessary.

Traveling Dollhouse
with Furniture

Dollhouse, ready to travel.

At last! A gadabout, stowaway dollhouse crammed with all the fun and furniture and imagination that dollhouses are famous for. It knocks down completely for car trips with kids or stays at Grandmother's house stashed neatly away between grandchildren-ly visits. Floor and walls are ⅜-inch plywood. Contents are made of balsa wood, glue, cardboard, or found objects.

You'll have as much fun making this house and its contents as the children will when they play with it. Save this one for a long weekend — and be sure to get everything you need ahead of time.

119

Kitchen

Living room

Grown-ups' room

Children's room

HOUSE

Floor Size: 27" x 27".

Materials:

> ⅜" plywood, two 11" x 27" pieces for walls, four 13½"
> squares for floors
> primer
> water- or oil-base paint or paper (self-adhesive or gift wrap)
> rubber cement (if using gift wrap)
> single-edge razor blade or mat knife
> sandpaper
> wood veneer strips and wood glue (optional)

Starting at center of one long edge of one wall piece, with saw cut out 5½"-long notch ⅜" wide (Diagram 1). Repeat on other wall piece. Test-fit the two wall pieces together by sliding the notched edges together crosswise.

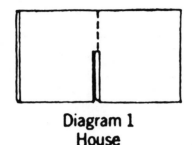

Diagram 1
House

Sand all cut edges and prime all surfaces. Paint floors and walls or cover with paper and veneer strips. See To Cover Floors and Walls, below.

Floors: Cut paper 18″ square. Glue a floor to center of wrong side of paper. Notch corners and fold excess paper to wrong side of floor. *Note:* We used self-adhesive paper with wood-grain pattern.

Walls: Cut paper slightly larger than wall section. Line up one edge of paper with center line (broken line on Diagram 1) on wall panel and glue paper to wall. Trim away excess paper with razor or knife. *Note:* We used shiny self-adhesive paper in kitchen, printed gift wrap in bedrooms, one painted wall and one wall covered with veneer strips in living room.

To Cover Floors and Walls: *Self-Adhesive-Paper Method:* Follow manufacturer's directions. *Dry-Mount Method* (for gift wrap or other nonsticking paper): Brush a coat of rubber cement over both surfaces to be joined. Let dry. Place a piece of plain paper on plywood, leaving about 1″ of plywood exposed along top edge. Press sticky side of gift wrap to exposed section of plywood. As you slowly slide the plain paper down, smooth the gift wrap to the plywood inch by inch as it becomes exposed. Work slowly and carefully. *Veneer-Strip Method:* We used flexible wood trim by Weldwood, which comes in paper-thin 1″-wide rolls. You will need about 7 feet for one wall. (Self-adhesive paper with wood-grain design, cut in strips, can be substituted.) Follow photograph for placement; cut strips to form chevron design and glue; allow 1/16″ space between strips for accent lines.

Materials for Furniture:
    unless otherwise specified, use ⅛″-thick balsa wood
    white glue
    acrylic paints

KITCHEN

Cabinet next to Stove:

Materials:
balsa wood
three 1½″ x 2″ matchboxes
scraps of printed fabric
10 map tacks
shiny-colored self-adhesive paper

Following Diagram 2, from balsa wood cut two A pieces 2⅛″ x 3¼″, one B piece 2⅝″ x 4½″, one C piece 2⅛″ x 4½″, two D pieces 4″ x 4¾″, and one E piece 2⅛″ x 4¾″. Glue fabric over one side and edges of D-1 piece. Glue all pieces together as

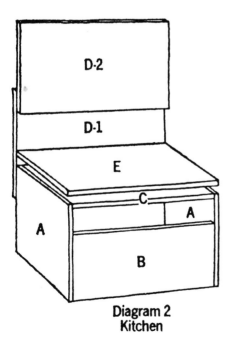

Diagram 2
Kitchen

shown on diagram, gluing E flush on top of C (space between pieces on diagram is to clarify procedure). Slide matchboxes into opening above B and glue to bottom of C and sides of A's. Cover A, B, and D-2 pieces with shiny paper. Cut four balsa-wood cabinet doors 1" x 2⅝" and three doors 1½" x 3½". Cover one side of each with shiny paper. Glue four small doors to B and three larger doors to D-2. Insert map tacks in doors and drawers for knobs. Drawers really work.

Cabinet next to Refrigerator:

Materials:
balsa wood
scrap of printed fabric
shiny-colored self-adhesive paper
10 map tacks
scrap shiny silver paper
2 screws and 1 long nail

Following Diagram 3, from balsa wood cut one A piece 2⅛" x 3¼", one B piece 3¼" x 8¼", one C piece 2¼" x 8¼", two D pieces 4" x 8¼", one E piece 2⅛" x 4", and one F piece 2⅜" x

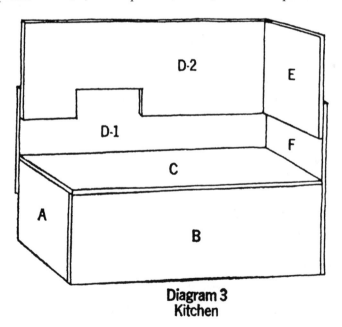

Diagram 3
Kitchen

6¾". Measure 1¾" from corner along one long edge of D-2 piece and cut notch 1¾" long x 1½" deep. Glue fabric over one side and edges of D-1 piece. Glue all pieces together as shown on diagram and cover A, B, D-2, and E pieces with shiny paper. Cut three balsa-wood cabinet doors 1⅜" x 3", four doors 1⅜" x 3⅝", and two doors 1⅜" x 2". Cover one side of each with shiny paper. Glue smallest doors above notch on D-2, 3⅝"-long doors to remainder of D and to E, and 3-long doors to B. Cut ½" x 2¾" balsa shelf and edge-glue at base of notch on D-2. Cut silver-paper "sink," round corners, and glue to counter C. Insert screw partway in C for knobs. Bend nail into curve and insert between screws for faucet. Insert map tacks in doors.

Stove:

Materials:
large shiny white box top and 2¼" x 3¼" x 1" deep box top
scrap of silver self-adhesive paper
4 metal washers
4 map tacks

From large box top cut two 2¼" x 3½" sides, one each 3" x 3½" front and back, one 2¼" x 3¼" top, and one 3¼" x 6¾" upright back piece. Glue first five pieces together. Cover 4" on one side of upright with silver paper. Glue upright to back of stove. Cut 2¼"-square oven door and ½" x 2¼" grill door; glue to stove front. Cut 1" x 2" silver paper and glue to center of oven door. Slide top of upright into inverted small box top and glue. Glue washers to stove top for burners. Add map tacks.

Refrigerator:

Materials:
large shiny white box top
balsa-wood trim
scrap silver paper

From box top cut two 2½" x 7" sides, one each 3½" x 7" front and back, and one each 2½" x 3¾" top and bottom. Glue pieces together to form closed box. Cut two doors and glue to front of refrigerator. Glue two balsa-wood strips to doors. Cut tiny silver rectangle and glue to top corner of one door.

Table:

Materials:
3½"-diameter plastic tape container
round plastic pill jar (about 2" diameter)
two 1¼" dowel rounds
two sturdy 1¾"-long springs
2 pill-container caps
clear cement for plastic
scrap of double-faced masking or foam tape

Remove top from large pill jar. Glue tape container to top of jar. Paint dowel rounds and springs for stool seats and pedestals. Glue a seat to each spring. To form stands for stools, stick tape inside caps and press ends of springs into tape.

Crocheted Kitchen Mat: *Size:* About 2¾" x 1¾".

Materials:
5 yards cotton cord
aluminum crochet hook size K (or Canadian hook No. 4)

Starting at one long edge, ch 9. **1st row:** Sc in 2nd ch from hook and in each ch across; ch 1, turn. **2nd row:** Sc in each sc across; ch 1, turn. Repeat last row 3 times more. Break off.

Cord Hanging: *Size:* 6" long

Materials:
cotton cord
four ⅜"-diameter wooden beads
one ⅝"-diameter wooden bead
white glue
2" piece ⅛"-diameter dowel

Knot lengths of cord over dowel and work macramé knots or braid lengths, adding beads as desired.

Broom: Remove some straw from a whiskbroom and glue around a 4½" dowel. Then wind tightly with wire or string.

Accessories: Spice containers and napkin holders are tiny seed-bead containers. For cans, jars, bottles, etc., cover scraps of balsa wood with food labels cut from magazines. Napkins and place mats are scraps of fabric (fringe place mats if desired). Plates are buttons. Other accessories are dollhouse miniatures sold in novelty and toy stores.

LIVING ROOM

Fireplace:

Materials:
mat board
¼" x ½" balsa-wood stripping
sixteen ⅜"-square ceramic tiles
antique gold and brown self-adhesive paper

Cut the following pieces from mat board: two 1¼" x 5" sides, one 1½" x 5" top piece, one 5" x 5" front piece with 1¾" x 2" cut out for fireplace, one 2⅜" x 5" floor piece, and one 5" x 5" back piece. From balsa-wood stripping also cut two 1½" and one 5½" pieces to face top edge of mantel. Cover one side of back piece and floor piece with self-adhesive paper. Assemble fireplace with glue as in photograph, leaving floor piece unattached. Arrange and glue ceramic tiles around fireplace cutout. Glue balsa stripping around top edge for mantel.

Needlepoint Picture over Fireplace: *Size:* 3⅜" x 3½", framed.

Materials:
6" square piece of needlepoint canvas with 10 meshes per
   inch
small amounts needlepoint yarn in different colors
tapestry needle
balsa wood for backing and frame

Following chart, work walk in half cross-stitch and the rest of the picture in bargello stitch. To avoid confusion, only a few bargello stitches for grass and sky are shown on chart. The different patterns shown on stitch symbols represent different colors.

Trim canvas, leaving ¼" seam allowance all around. Cut balsa wood to same size and glue to canvas. Cut strips of balsa wood for frame. Paint frame and glue to right side of seam allowance. Attach to wall with hidden double-faced tape.

Needlepoint Picture

Half cross-stitch

Bargello Lion Pillow
Painted Stone Turtle

Fabric Anemones
Eggshell Tulips
Roses from Cans

Bargello Glasses Case
Embroidered Pincushions

Hanging Planter:

Materials:
thimble
scrap jute
small bunch of dried flowers
thin flexible wire

Paint thimble if desired. Cut four lengths of jute; knot together at one end. Separate strands into pairs and tie square knots in each pair (1 and 2, 3 and 4). Separate strands again, pairing 1 and 4, 2 and 3; tie square knots 1" from first set. Separate, tie square knots with 1 and 2, 3 and 4, 1" from second set. Separate, tie square knots with 1 and 4, 2 and 3, 1" from third set. Fold loose ends into loop for hanging and bind ends to main body of cords with wire. Insert thimble, fill with flowers.

Chair:

Materials:
3/8" dowel
balsa wood
scrap upholstery fabric for cushion or see Note below
absorbent cotton for stuffing
1" x 2½" piece thin cardboard covered with wood-grain
     paper

Note: We made a simple geometric-design needlepoint cushion for our chair.

For chair cut two 2½" front and two 4½" back legs from 3/8" dowel. Cut notches for chair seat ¼" down from one end on front legs and 2¼" down from one end on back legs. Cut 2" square of balsa wood for chair seat and assemble as in photograph with glue. Glue paper-covered cardboard piece in place for chair back.

For cushion cut two 2¼" squares of fabric. Stitch, leaving opening to stuff. Turn, stuff, and close.

Beanbag Chair:

Materials:
scrap fabric-backed vinyl
rice for stuffing

Using compass, make a pattern for 2"-diameter hexagon for top piece, 3"-diameter hexagon for bottom piece, and 4" x 2¼" rectangle tapered slightly at each end for sides; cut out. Using patterns, cut one each top and bottom pieces and six side pieces, adding ¼" seam allowance all around. Stitch side pieces together along long edges to form six-sided ring. With right sides facing, pin top and bottom pieces in place. Stitch, leaving half of bottom open. Turn, fill chair with rice, and close opening.

Large Shag Rug: *Size:* 5½" x 6½".

Materials:
1 ounce knitting worsted
aluminum crochet hook size G (or Canadian hook No. 9)
26" piece ⅜"-wide white grosgrain ribbon

Starting at one long edge, ch 25. **1st row (wrong side):** Make lp about 1½" long around first two fingers of left hand. Insert hook in 2nd ch from hook and draw a bit of the lp through the stitch; remove fingers from lp, y o hook and draw through to complete sc (lp st made), make a lp st in each st across chain; ch 1, turn. **2nd row (right side):** Sc in front lp only of each st across; ch 1, turn. **3rd row:** Work lp st in each st across; ch 1, turn. Repeat last 2 rows 6 times more. Break off. Cut lps to form shag. Sew grosgrain ribbon to edges of rug on wrong side.

Coffee Table:

Materials:
mat board
chrome self-adhesive paper

Cut the following pieces from mat board: two 1⅝" x 2⅛" side pieces, two 1⅝" x 3⅛" front and back pieces, and one 2½" x 3½" tabletop. Cover one side of each piece with chrome self-adhesive paper. Assemble sides, front, and back with glue for base; center and glue top in place.

Sofa:

Materials:
mat board and wicker or wood-tone design self-adhesive
    paper
scraps of fabric for cushions
absorbent cotton for stuffing

Cut the following pieces from mat board: two 1⅞" x 2" pieces
for sides, two 1⅞" x 5½" pieces for back and front, and one 2¼"
x 5½" piece for seat. Cover one side of each piece with
self-adhesive paper for bottom structure of sofa. Assemble
with glue. From mat board cut two 1⅝" x 2¼" pieces for arms
and one 1⅝" x 5¾" piece for backrest. Cover both sides of each
piece and glue in C-shape around bottom structure. For cushions cut eight 3¼" x 3¾" pieces from fabric. For each cushion,
stitch two pieces together, leaving opening. Turn, stuff, and
close.

Floor Lamp:

Materials:
scrap 1- or 2-ply Bristol board
shaped 1⅜"-long bead
6" length ¼" dowel
scrap chrome self-adhesive paper

From Bristol board cut 1⅝" x 7" strip and a 2"-diameter circle.
Make 2"-diameter cylinder from strip, gluing overlapped ends.
Cover cylinder and circle with self-adhesive paper; glue circle
to one end of cylinder for lampshade. Cover dowel with
self-adhesive paper. Glue one end of dowel in bead, then
center and glue shade on opposite end.

Accessories: Tiny brass candlesticks, andirons, wineglasses,
and painted pottery jug from novelty or toy stores. Shallow,
clear plastic box tops, one round and one rectangular, for
trays. They can be decorated with self-adhesive paper. Rectangular tray filled with a collection of tiny shells, pine cones,
and beans. Round end table is an empty spool, turned on end.
Dried flowers are in a brass-plated chair stabilizer turned on
end. Small basket from novelty store holds bought paper
flowers.

GROWN-UPS' BEDROOM

Bed:

Materials:
balsa wood
5½' length ¼"-diameter dowel
four ¾"-diameter wooden beads
scraps of printed fabrics
1 yard 2½"-wide cotton lace
cotton batting for stuffing
½ yard 1"-wide cotton lace
scrap of white fabric
12" length ¼"-wide rickrack
30" length ½"-wide rickrack

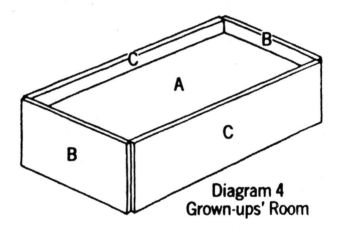

Diagram 4
Grown-ups' Room

Following Diagram 4, cut from balsa wood: one A piece 4" x 7⅜", two B pieces 2" x 4⅛", and two C pieces 2" x 7⅜". For canopy cut one piece 4¼" x 7⅝". Glue A, B's, and C's together as shown in diagram, positioning A ½" below top edges of B's and C's and leaving notches at corners as shown. Cut dowel into the following lengths: four 7" bedposts, two 5" head and foot crossbars, two 7⅜" side canopy frames, and two 4¼" end canopy frames. Paint bed, dowels, beads, and canopy. Glue bedposts into notches at corners of bed, and glue crossbars at head and foot.

Gather 2½"-wide lace to fit around canopy. Glue ½" of gathered edge to underside of canopy. Glue dowel frames around underside of canopy against lace, and glue top ends of bedposts at canopy corners. Glue ½" rickrack around top of canopy and add four beads at corners.

For bed flounce cut two strips each 3" x 10" and 3" x 6" from printed fabric. Glue hems on one long side of each strip. Gather opposite edges to fit sides and ends of bed; glue to inside edges of bed top.

For quilt, cut printed fabric 5¾" x 9¼" for lining. Make quilt top from fifteen pieced squares of assorted prints, cutting squares 2¼" and making ¼" seams. Assemble squares three wide by five long. Place a layer of batting between quilt top and lining, turn under ½" seams around edges, and topstitch layers together. Topstitch around each square for quilting.

For pillow, cut two pieces white fabric 3" x 4". Stitch together, making ¼" seams and leaving one end open. Turn and stuff. Turn in raw edges and sew. Gather 1"-wide lace to fit around pillow; topstitch. Glue narrow rickrack around stitching.

Dresser:

Materials:
balsa wood
2' length ¼"-square balsa-wood stripping
four ⅝"-diameter and eight ⁷⁄₁₆"-diameter wooden beads
wood-grain self-adhesive paper
two 1½" x 2" oval mirrors

From balsa wood cut two 1¾" x 3" sides, one each 3" x 4¾" front and back, and one 1⅞" x 5" top. Cover one side and all edges of each piece with self-adhesive paper. Glue sides to front and back. Glue top in place (it will overlap front ⅛"). From balsa wood cut four 1¼" x 2" drawer fronts and cover one side of each with self-adhesive paper. Glue to front of dresser. Cut balsa-wood strip into four 6" lengths for posts. Cover each with self-adhesive paper. Glue each mirror between two posts. Glue post units to back of dresser. Paint beads and glue four large ones to bottom corners of dresser. Glue the others to drawers and top of posts.

Chair:

Materials:
12-ounce cardboard frozen juice container
scrap of fabric
cotton batting

Starting 1¾" up from bottom (closed end of container) mark 1" horizontal line for seat front; then, working from each end of line, mark a curved line to form 4½"-high seat back. Cut away excess. Mark and cut out heart design in chair back. Cut and glue cardboard circle to fit opening tightly for seat. Paint.

For pillow, cut two 3½"-diameter fabric circles. Stitch together with ¼" seams, leaving 1" opening. Turn and stuff. Close opening.

Rug: *Size:* About 6½" x 5½".

Materials:
knitting worsted, small amount each light blue (color B), white (W), red (R), and navy (N)
knitting needles, 1 pair No. 6

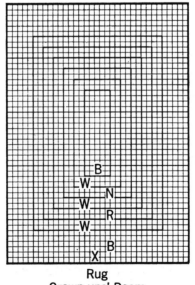

Rug
Grown-ups' Room

Starting at one end (X on chart), with color B cast on 35 sts. Work even in stockinette st (k 1 row, p 1 row) for 6 rows. **7th row (right side):** K 5, drop B but do not break off; attach W and k 25, drop W; attach another ball of B and k 5. **8th row:** P 5 B, p 25 W, p 5 B.

Following chart, continue in stockinette st, changing colors as indicated. Bind off. Block.

Accessories: Plant pedestal is upended pill container covered with self-adhesive paper. Plant is bits of dried flowers in a painted thimble. Clock is picture of a clock cut from a magazine and glued to balsa wood. Basket is a small basket from novelty store filled with dried grasses. Photograph on dresser is tiny picture pasted to foil-covered rectangle braced in back with a cardboard triangle. Lamp, comb, and brush are from toy and novelty stores.

CHILDREN'S BEDROOM

Hat Rack:

Materials:
From Tinkertoy set:
one 1⅜"-diameter disk for base and one 1⅜"-diameter disk with side holes for top
eight 1" and one 5⅜" dowel piece for spokes and pole
tiny straw hat

Assemble hat rack as in photograph.

Bunk Beds:

Materials:
¼"-square balsa-wood stripping
balsa wood
scraps of print fabrics for coverlets and pillows
1 yard ¼" rickrack
scrap yarn
absorbent cotton for stuffing

Cut and paint four 6" pieces of ¼"-square balsa wood stripping for bedposts. From ⅛"-thick balsa wood cut the following pieces: two 3½" x 7⅛" pieces for mattress boards, four 1" x 7⅛" side pieces, two 1" x 3⅝" footboards, and two 2" x 3⅝" headboards. Following photograph, assemble pieces with glue to form two open boxes so that head and footboard edges are extended slightly beyond corners to form notches (see corners on Diagram 4 for parents' bed). Paint head- and footboard. Glue posts in notches at corners to join beds bunk-style.

For each coverlet cut two 5½" x 8½" pieces from fabric scraps. Stitch pieces together, leaving opening for stuffing. Turn, stuff lightly, and close opening. To tuft, scatter small stitches with yarn over coverlet, tying four 1½" lengths of yarn in each stitch.

For pillows cut two 3¾" x 4¾" pieces from fabric. Stitch and stuff as for coverlets. Trim with rickrack.

Desk-Chest Unit:

Materials:
balsa wood
six ½"-diameter wooden beads
two 1½" x 2" matchboxes

For chest cut the following pieces from balsa wood: two 2⅛" squares for top and bottom, four 2¼" x 6" side pieces, and four 1¼" x 1¾" drawer fronts. Assemble pieces with glue to form closed box. Paint drawer fronts and glue in place. Add a painted bead to each for knob.

For desk cut the following pieces from balsa wood: one 2⅛" x 3" top piece and one 2⅛" x 2½" side piece. Paint matchbox ends for drawers (be careful not to paint them closed, as you should be able to push them in and out later). Glue drawers to underside of desktop piece; add painted beads for knobs. Glue top and side to form L-shape; glue to chest.

Desk Lamp:

Materials:
one 1¼"-long shaped wooden bead
one ¾"-diameter wooden bead
one 1"-diameter fluted plastic candy cup

Glue ¾" bead to one end of shaped bead, then center and glue candy cup over ¾" bead for shade.

Desk Stool:

Materials:
one small wooden block
scrap fabric
absorbent cotton

Paint block. Paint a circle on each side. For cushion cut two 2"-diameter circles of fabric. Stitch together, leaving opening to stuff. Turn, stuff, and close opening. Work a single stitch through center to tuft.

Bulletin Board:

Materials:
2⅛" x 3¼" piece balsa wood
1⅞" square ⅛" cork or corrugated board
tiny picture from magazine
map tacks
double-faced tape

Paint balsa wood and decorate along top with picture. Glue cork centered under picture and insert a few map tacks. Attach to wall with tape.

Braided Rug:

Materials:
6 yards each pink, red, and yellow yarn
matching thread

Cut each yarn length in half. Knot all six strands together at one end. Pairing like colors, braid yarn. Beginning at knotted end, coil and sew braid until rug measures about 8" in diameter.

Easel:

Materials:
⅛"-square balsa-wood stripping
1/16"-thick mat board
map tacks
crayon drawing

From stripping cut four 4¼" lengths, mitering one end of each piece. Assemble lengths to form two V-shapes. Also from stripping cut two 1¼" crosspieces to brace V-shapes. Miter ends of crosspieces to fit; glue in place. Legs now form A-shape. From mat board cut two 2¾" squares. Following photograph, glue one to each side of easel. Cut stripping into two 2⅝" pieces and glue one to bottom edge of each board for crayon tray. Pin crayon drawing to a board with map tacks.

Toys and Accessories: Mirror is 2"-round mirror glued to flower-shaped gift tag and attached to wall with double-faced tape. Basket is tiny purchased basket filled with dried flowers. Picture is colored photograph cut from magazine and glued to painted balsa wood. Train is shaped scraps of balsa wood and bits of dowel glued together; wheels are painted wooden beads and cars are joined with tiny hooks and screw eyes. Dollhouse is a painted box top with cardboard dividers and roof.

Easter Eggs

The cleverest designs are sometimes the easiest to make — like these darling jackrabbits-in-the-box and appliquéd eggs.

The bunnies are simply blown eggs, with paper ears and button hats glued on, mounted on white-painted springs. The little boxes are handmade from cardboard and filled with Easter grass.

The trimmed eggs are also blown, then dyed and decorated with cotton appliqués, rickrack, and signal dots. It's a snap to personalize them with self-adhesive letters or with transfer type, and they'd look equally pretty nestled in a basket or hung from thread as an eggs-traordinary mobile.

Materials:
> eggs
> dye
> white glue
> embroidered appliqué motifs
> rickrack
> signal dots
> transfer and press-on type
> light cardboard
> white and colored paper
> two ¾"-diameter springs about 4" high
> 1" red metal caps or buttons
> white paint
> felt-tipped markers in black and red
> rubber cement
> Easter grass

Empty all eggshells by punching or snipping two holes at opposite ends (or sides) and blowing out contents. Holes can be used for hanging or concealed with trimming. For coloring, use any Easter egg dye as directed by the manufacturer.

On trimmed eggs, follow photograph to glue embroidery appliqués and frame them with narrow rickrack. Self-sticking signal dots border the rickrack on purple and white eggs; transfer type and press-on letters spell out individual names.

For bunny eggs, follow photograph to cut 2"-long paper ears with tabs for attaching; with markers, draw features and color ears. Glue tabs to head; add red cap. Paint spring white and glue to egg.

For box, follow diagram to cut lightweight cardboard. Score along dotted lines and bend sides upward and lid backward.

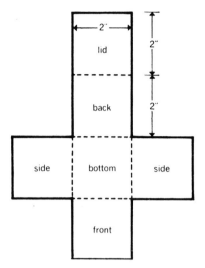

Cut stiff yellow paper, one piece to line the two sides and front, another piece to line back and lid; put aside. Cut pink or orange paper to cover outside of box and lid, adding ¼" for turn-in at top and ½" allowance at bottom.

Assemble box with white glue and hold with rubber bands until dry. Trimming paper corners at an angle, cement colored paper to outside; cement lining pieces to inside, covering turn-in allowance.

Glue bunny on spring inside box; fill with paper grass.

PET
PROJECTS

Sasha Sleeper

Materials:

corrugated carton to fit your cat (our carton
measures 14″ x 18″ x 12″)
1¾ yards 36″-wide burlap

Sasha Sleeper is a burlap-covered corrugated carton with a fabric
lining and pillow. The ball and scratch post are crocheted of cotton
yarn.

1½ yards 36"-wide gingham for lining and pillow
Dacron polyester or foam rubber to stuff pillow
ball of natural jute wrapping cord
ball of thinner black jute cord
black self-stick tape
Velcro fastening to close box
white glue and brush

To Cover Box: Tape bottom of box closed. Cut 7"-diameter hole in end of box. Cut away end flaps at top of box, leaving side flaps for closing. Cut burlap 2" wider than box, front to back, and long enough to fit side of box and both sides of flap, extending 3" into box beyond flap and 1" under bottom.

Pour glue into bowl and thin a bit with water. Turn burlap in 1" at sides and glue to form neat edges. Brush glue on surface of box to be covered and smooth burlap in place. Cover opposite side of box and other flap in same manner, allowing extra fabric for a 2" overlap at edge of flap to close top of box.

To cover ends of box, cut burlap 2" wider, as before, and long enough to fold 2" over top rim and 1" under bottom. Finish side edges and glue to box. Cut 6"-diameter hole over hole on box. Clip edges; fold and glue to inside. Tape edges on box with black tape as shown in photograph. Glue two or three strips Velcro to flap and matching edge for closing.

To Line Box: Line sides and ends of inside of box with gingham pieces cut 1" wider on all edges than side to be covered. Turn under all edges and topstitch. Glue to inside of box, spreading glue on seam allowances only. Cut 6" hole over hole as before. Clip edges, turn to inside, and glue or hand-sew.

Pillow: Cut two pieces gingham to fit bottom of box, adding ½" seam allowance on all edges. With right sides facing, stitch three sides. Turn, stuff, and close opening. Tuft with a stitch here and there to hold stuffing in place.

To Decorate: Cut nine 1-yard lengths natural jute. Tie together at one end. Braid lengths into neat, flat braid to fit around hole. Clip ends and glue braid around hole. Untie other end, overlap first end, and glue.

Cut strips of natural jute to form cat's name; glue over hole. Outline with strips of black jute.

Scratch Post and Ball

SIZE: Post is 20″ long x 3″ wide. Ball is about 2½″ in diameter.

MATERIALS:

    Craft Cord No. 18 (heavy, tightly twisted cord, available in hobby shops and craft-supply stores), 1 (120-yard) ball each toast and black and 1 (60-yard) ball natural

    20″ piece 2 x 3 lumber (or desired size)

    aluminum crochet hook size H (or international size 5.00 mm) *or the size that will give you the correct gauge*

    large-eye tapestry needle

    stuffing for ball

GAUGE: 3 sc = 1″; 3 rows = 1″.

SCRATCH POST

Long Piece: With toast ch 31 to measure about 10″ (or if lumber is a different size, work a chain long enough to fit around lumber). **1st row:** Sc in 2nd ch from hook and in each ch across (30 sc); ch 1, turn. **2nd row:** Sc in each sc across; ch 1, turn. Repeat 2nd row until piece measures 6″ from beg; do not ch 1 at end of last row. Break off toast, attach natural; ch 1, turn. Work 1 row sc with natural. Mark this row for right side of work. Always change colors on right side of work. Continue in sc and work in following colors: Work 3 rows more with natural, 5″ with black, ending with a wrong-side row, 4 rows with natural, and 6½″ with toast or until piece measures 20″ from beg (or until piece fits length of lumber). Break off.

    End Pieces (make 2): With toast ch 11 (or work a chain long enough to fit across width of lumber). Work even on 10 sc until piece measures 2″ from beg (or will cover depth of lumber). Break off.

FINISHING: Wrap striped piece around lumber. With toast sew lengthwise seam. Sew end pieces in place.

BALL

With toast ch 4. Join with sl st to form ring. **1st rnd:** Work 7 sc in ring. **2nd rnd:** Work 2 sc in each sc around (14 sc). **3rd rnd:** * Sc in next sc, 2 sc in next sc. Repeat from * around (21 sc); join with sl st to 1st sc. Break off. **4th rnd:** With natural work sc in each sc around (21 sc); join and break off. With black work even in sc for 2 rnds. Join and break off at end of 2nd rnd. With natural work even in sc for 1 rnd; join and break off. **8th rnd:** With toast work even in sc (21 sc). Stuff ball firmly and continue to stuff as you work. **9th rnd (dec rnd):** * Sc in next sc, draw up lp in each of next 2 sc, y o, and draw through all 3 lps on hook (1 sc dec). Repeat from * around (14 sc). **10th rnd (dec rnd):** * Dec 1 sc over next 2 sc. Repeat from * around (7 sc). **11th rnd:** Repeat from * on last rnd 3 times. Break off. Sew opening closed.

Snug Dog Sweater

SIZES: 12½" [15"] from neck to tail.

MATERIALS:

sport-weight yarn, 4 ounces red

knitting needles, 1 pair No. 5 and 1 set (4) double-pointed No. 5 (or English needles No. 8), *or the size that will give you the correct gauge*

GAUGE: Rib pattern when stretched: 5 sts = 1"; 9 rows = 1".

TURTLENECK: Starting at neck edge, cast 72 sts evenly onto 3 dp needles. Join, being careful not to twist sts. **1st rnd:** * K 2, p 2. Repeat from * around. Repeat last rnd until piece measures 4" [5"] from beg.

To Divide Work: **Next row:** Work in k 2, p 2 ribbing across 1st 16 sts for underpanel; divide remaining 56 sts onto 2 st holders.

UNDERPANEL: Working in rows from now on, work even in k 2, p 2 ribbing on 16 sts only for 1" [1½"]. Inc 1 st at beg and end of every row 6 times, working added sts in ribbing (28 sts). Mark beg and end of last row. Work even in ribbing on 28 sts until piece measures 9½" [11"] from cast-on row. Bind off in ribbing.

TOP SECTION (BACK): Work in rows as follows: Place the 56 sts from st holders onto single-pointed needle. Attach yarn and k across, increasing 10 sts as evenly spaced as possible (66 sts).

Back pattern: **1st row (wrong side):** (K 1, p 1) 6 times; k 2, p 6; * k 2, (p 1, k 1) twice; p 1, k 2 *; p 8. Repeat from * to * once; p 6, k 2; (p 1, k 1) 6 times. **2nd row:** (P 1, k 1) 6 times; p 2, k 6; * p 2, (k 1, p 1) twice; k 1, p 2 *; k 8. Repeat from * to * once; k 6, p 2; (k 1, p 1) 6 times. Repeat last 2 rows once more, then 1st row once again.

6th row (6-st cable row): (P 1, k 1) 6 times; p 2; sl next 3 sts onto dp needle and hold in back of work, k next 3 sts from dp needle (left cross made over 6 sts); * p 2, (k 1, p 1) twice; k 1, p 2 *; k 8. Repeat from * to * once; work a left cross over next 6 sts, p 2; (k 1, p 1) 6 times. **7th row:** Repeat 1st row.

8th row (8-st cable row): (P 1, k 1) 6 times; p 2, k 6; * p 2, (k 1, p 1) twice; k 1, p 2 *; sl next 4 sts onto dp needle and hold in back of work, k next 4 sts, k 4 sts from dp needle (left cross made over 8 sts). Repeat from * to * once; k 6, p 2, (k 1, p 1) 6 times. Repeat 1st and 2nd rows for pattern and, *at the same time,* work left crosses as before every 6th row on 6-st cable and every 8th row on 8-st cable until section measures 9" [11"]. Then work 1 row in k 2, p 2 ribbing, decreasing 10 sts evenly spaced across (56 sts). Continue in k 2, p 2 ribbing for 1½". Bind off loosely in ribbing. Piece should measure about 14½" [17½"] from cast-on row.

FRONT LEGS: Leaving opening for front legs, join side edges of underpanel to side edges of top section as follows: Starting at marker, sew each seam from marker to end (bound-off edge) of underpanel. Using dp needles and working in rounds, pick up and k 32 sts on 3 needles around each leg opening. Work even in k 2, p 2 ribbing for 2". Bind off in ribbing.

HIND-LEG STRAPS (make 2): Lengthwise tube forms each strap. Starting at one end of tube, cast on 8 sts. **1st row:** * K 1, bring yarn to front of work, sl 1, pass yarn to back of work. Repeat from * across. Repeat 1st row for 7" [8"]. K 2 tog and bind off. Sew one end of a tube to last row of top section and the other end ½" from joining of underpanel and top section. Sew other tube on other side of coat.

Needlepoint Name Collar

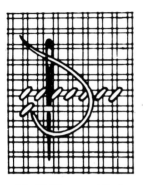

Half Cross-stitch

Size: About 7/8" wide; length is adjustable.

Materials:

scrap of needlepoint canvas with 12 spaces per inch (see directions below, to determine amount)

Persian-type needlepoint and crewel yarn, small amounts each yellow, orange, and blue

7/8"-wide orange grosgrain ribbon

snap fastener

matching sewing thread

tapestry needle

sheet of graph paper (any size)

Measure dog's neck. Canvas should measure 2" wide by dog's neck measurement plus 1¾" for overlap. Fold masking tape over canvas edges to prevent raveling. Baste two lines (each about ½" from a long edge) across canvas to mark the center 10 spaces used to make the collar. Baste two more lines ½" in from each end. Make a paper pattern to correspond to the basted rectangle on canvas.

Using alphabet (see diagram), draw dog's name on graph paper, allowing 1 space between letters (note that M and W are 1 space wider than other letters). Try pattern on dog and, allowing for ¾" snap overlap, mark where you want dog's name (count number of spaces used for name on graph; each space equals 1 stitch; 12 stitches equal 1").

Following alphabet, pattern diagram, and half-cross-stitch diagram, work name at marked place on canvas. Work two orange rows before first letter (see chart) and after last letter

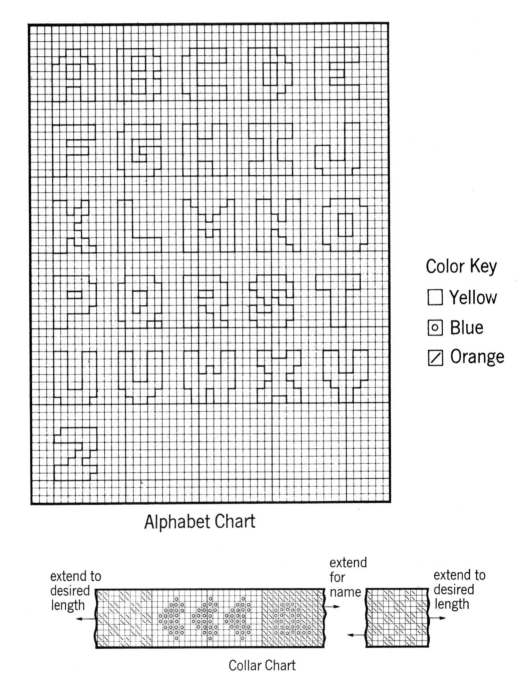

Alphabet Chart

Color Key

☐ Yellow
⊙ Blue
⊘ Orange

extend to desired length

extend for name

extend to desired length

Collar Chart

and one row between letters. Letters should be centered so that two orange stitches are on each side. (*Note:* If name contains *M* or *W*, make two orange stitches to the left and one stitch to the right of the letter.) After name is completed, work heart and checkerboard patterns, following diagram.

Block collar; trim canvas edges and press under. Cut ribbon to length of collar plus ½". Folding raw ends under ¼", topstitch ribbon in place. Sew snap to collar.

Posy Kitty Collar

SIZE: Collar is about ⅝" wide; length is adjustable.

MATERIALS:

D.M.C. pearl cotton No. 5, 1 (10-gram, 53-yard) ball each turquoise No. 518, red No. 321, pink No. 335, light orange No. 742, and yellow No. 445

steel crochet hook No. 5

Popcorn Band: With turquoise crochet chain that will fit comfortably around cat's neck. **1st row (right side):** Sc in 2nd ch from hook, * in next ch work popcorn as follows: (y o, insert hook in ch and draw up lp, y o and draw through 2 lps on hook) 6 times, y o and draw through 6 lps on hook, y o and draw through remaining 2 lps, sc in each of next 2 ch. Repeat from * across. Break off.

Edging: **1st rnd:** Make lp on hook with pink. With right side facing you, work sc completely around popcorn band, being careful not to draw work in; join and break off. **2nd rnd:** Make lp on hook with orange. With right side facing you, sc in each sc across 1 long edge, 1 end, and other long edge. Do not break off; crochet about 2¼"-long chain; sl st in 1st orange sc (loop made). Break off.

Flower Clasp: Starting at center with yellow, ch 4. Join with sl st to form ring. **1st rnd:** Ch 1, work 10 sc in ring; join with sl st to 1st sc. **2nd rnd:** Ch 6, (skip next sc, dc in next sc, ch 3) 4 times, skip last sc; join with sl st to 3rd ch of ch 6 (5 ch-3 lps). Break off. **3rd rnd:** With orange work petal of sc, h dc, dc, h dc, and sc in each ch-3 lp; join to 1st sc. Break off. **4th rnd:** Hold flower with right side facing you. With pink sl st in back of work in sp between any 2 petals (fold petals forward to do this), * ch 4, sl st in back of work in next sp between 2 petals. Repeat from * around, ending with ch 4, sl st in 1st sl st (5 chains across backs of petals). **5th rnd:** In each lp work petal of sc, h dc, 2 dc, h dc, and sc; join. Break off. **6th rnd:** With red sl st in back of work in sp between any 2 petals, * ch 5, sl st in back of work in next sp between 2 petals. Repeat from * around, ending with ch 5; sl st in 1st sl st. **7th rnd:** In each lp work petal of sc, h dc, 3 dc, h dc, and sc; join. Break off. Sew to end of collar opposite loop.

AND SOMETHING
FOR YOU

Bargello Sunglasses Case

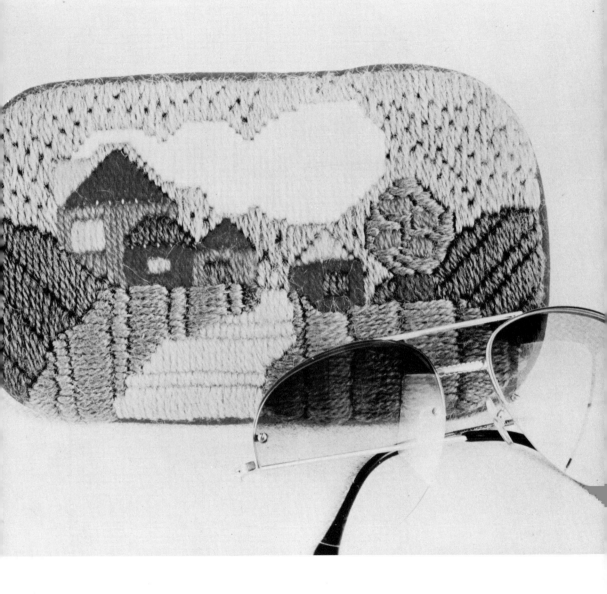

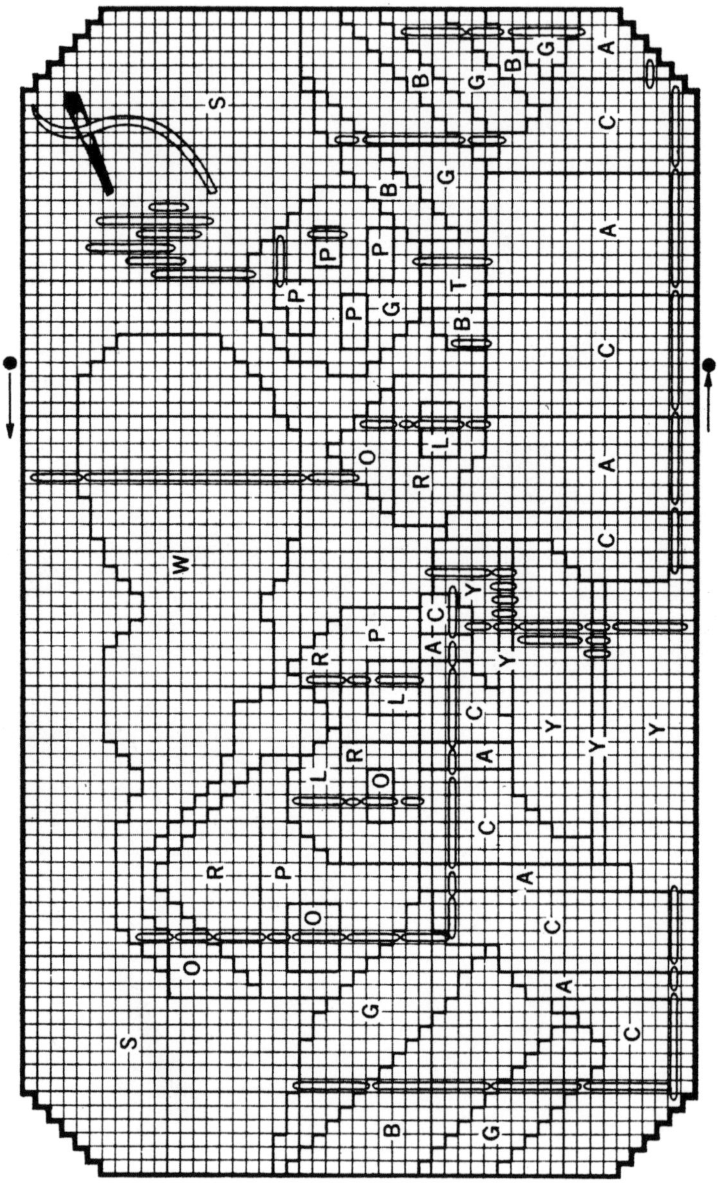

Color Key

A—Aqua

B—Royal Blue

C—Light Green

G—Medium Green

L—Lavender

O—Orange

P—Bright Pink

R—Red

S—Sky Blue

T—Brown

W—White

Y—Yellow-Gold

Size: About 4¼" x 7¼".

Materials:
   5¼" x 8¼" piece mono (single-mesh) needlepoint canvas
      with 12 meshes per inch
   3-ply Persian-type needlepoint and crewel yarn, 10 yards
      sky blue (color S), 5 yards each aqua (A), royal blue (B),
      light green (C), medium green (G), white (W), and
      yellow gold (Y)
   small amounts each lavender (L), orange (O), bright pink
      (P), red (R), and brown (T)
   6" x 17" piece red lining fabric
   6" x 9" piece blue velveteen backing
   ¾ yard red piping
   tapestry needle

To Prepare Canvas: Fold masking tape over edges to prevent
raveling.

With pencil or marker made especially for needlepoint, copy
outline of case on canvas (each square on chart equals 1 space
on canvas). Follow chart for color placement and sample
stitches on chart for stitch direction and length (for sky work
stitches at various lengths as shown). Use all three strands of
the three-ply yarn and make sure that the end of 1 st occupies
the same space as the end of the st directly above it to
completely cover canvas (see sample stitches on chart).

Finishing: Block canvas, if necessary. With raw edges facing
outward, sew piping to right side of canvas around edges of
needlepoint. Trim canvas to ½" seam allowance. Cut two
lining pieces and backing piece to size of canvas. With right
sides facing and piping sandwiched between, sew backing
piece to needlepoint between dots on chart, stitching in direction of arrows. Trim seams, clip curves, and turn. Sew lining
pieces together in same manner; turn. Insert lining in case, fold
in all raw edges, and blindstitch around open edges of case.

Embroidered Buttons

Run them down an old blouse or plunk a big one on a jeans pocket or shoulder bag. These are some of the gayest novelties — simple and fun to make, instant refreshers for last year's clothes or this year's basics, and a catchy gift idea. Attach a set to cardboard of the same color and you won't even want to gift-wrap. The designs use easy embroidery stitches on fabric that matches or contrasts with the garment being buttoned. Buttons good for covering are available at any notions counter.

Sizes: Button mold size 36 for the small buttons, $7/8$" in diameter; size 60 for the medium size, $1\frac{1}{2}$" in diameter; size 75 for the large one, $1\frac{7}{8}$" in diameter.

Materials:
 "Cover-your-own" button molds in desired size and
  quantity (available at most variety stores or notion
  departments)
 solid-color fabric to cover button molds: small amounts of
  crewel wool for embroidery in lilac (color A), scarlet (B),
  medium blue (C), purple (D), light green (E), royal blue
  (F), hot pink (G), kelly green (H), and orange (I)
 embroidery needle
 embroidery hoop, if desired
 dressmaker's carbon paper or regular carbon paper and
  tracing paper for transferring design

Note: If your fabric has a soil-release finish, you may find it difficult to transfer these designs. Instead, you will have to draw the design on the fabric with a pencil.

Shown here are just a few designs to decorate your buttons and a selection of embroidery stitches. You can use ours or make up your own — pick a motif from the print of your dress, spell out your name, etc. There are an infinite number of possibilities for making fun buttons.

GENERAL DIRECTIONS
It is better to transfer and embroider these designs on your fabric, then cut them apart. Following button-mold manufacturer's directions for size, with a pencil draw as many circles on

No. 1

No. 2

No. 3

No. 4

No. 5

No. 6

No. 7

No. 8

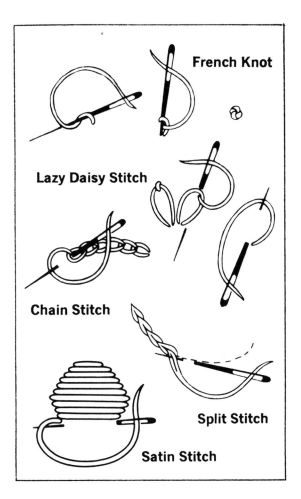

French Knot

Lazy Daisy Stitch

Chain Stitch

Split Stitch

Satin Stitch

the right side of fabric as required, being sure to leave enough fabric between circles to finish buttons.

Transferring Design: Copy design on tracing paper. Place carbon paper, with carbon side down, on fabric; then, centering design, place tracing paper, right side up, over carbon. With pointed instrument, such as a knitting needle, transfer designs, pressing firmly.

Embroidery: Use embroidery hoop if desired. Follow stitch diagrams for embroidery. Some flowers are worked in satin stitch, others in lazy daisy stitch. Leaves are worked in satin stitch and lazy daisy stitch. Use split stitch on large button for letters, also for stems on all buttons. Use chain stitch on medium-size buttons only. French knots are indicated by small circles.

Crewel wool can be separated into three strands of two-ply wool. Work your embroidery with various numbers of strands.

Small Buttons:
Nos. 1 and 2: Use E, F, G, and H.
No. 3: Use B, G, and H.
Nos. 4, 5, and 6: Use B, E, F, and G.
No. 7: Use B, F, and H.
No. 8: Use B, E, and G.

Medium-size Buttons: Use A, C, D, and I for all four.

Large Buttons: Use A, B, E, and I.

Finishing: After embroidery is completed, cut circles apart. Following manufacturer's directions, cover button molds.

Embroidered Pincushions

168

Each square = 1" square

BROWN PINCUSHION

You can easily finish one of these pretty pincushions in an evening. Make one for yourself and the others for gifts. You probably have everything you need for these projects in your scrapbasket.

Size: 4½" x 6½".

Materials:
    For each pincushion: 7½" x 11" piece cotton or linen
    small amount kapok or Dacron for stuffing
    tapestry needle
    embroidery hoop
    crewel yarn in assorted colors
    For brown pincushion we used olive, moss, and lime green, shades of brown and burnt orange, purple, gold, and brick red
    For blue pincushion we used moss green, gold, and shades of magenta, purple, and blue
    For red pincushion we used olive green, turquoise, and shades of red and orange

Each square = 1″ square

BLUE PINCUSHION

Each square = 1″ square

RED PINCUSHION

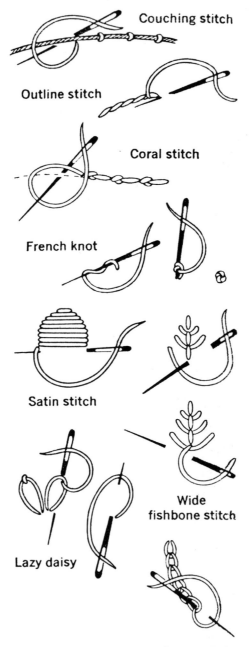

Couching stitch

Outline stitch

Coral stitch

French knot

Satin stitch

Wide
fishbone stitch

Lazy daisy

Chain stitch

To Prepare Fabric: For each pincushion, mark two rectangles 5½″ x 7½″ on fabric (½″ seam allowance included on all sides). Enlarge design according to directions on page 175. Center and transfer design using carbon paper placed face down on one piece of fabric.

Embroidery: The patterns are drawn to simulate embroidery stitches as much as possible. Small circles indicate French knots, chains of small ovals are chain stitch, larger ovals notched at one end with a straight line are lazy daisies, leaves marked A on blue pincushion are wide fishbone stitch. All other areas marked with heavy outlines are to be filled in with satin stitch. The fine lines show direction the satin stitches are to be worked. See stitch diagrams and follow photograph in color section for colors.

Finishing: With right sides facing, seam a plain and an embroidered piece together, leaving 2″ open for stuffing. Turn, stuff, and sew opening closed. Cut yarn to fit around seam. With contrasting color sewing thread, couch yarn in place.

Mesh Back-Tote

This mini-mesh back-tote that expands to carry all sorts of things, slings over shoulders from a long strap. It's mostly single and double crochet, and the work goes very quickly in Coats & Clark's Speed-Cro-Sheen.

SIZE: Tote bag measures 11" wide x 14" deep.

MATERIALS:

Coats & Clark's Speed-Cro-Sheen, 3 (100-yard) balls tango (orange) No.135 and 1 ball parakeet (turquoise) No. 132

steel crochet hook No. 00, *or the size that will give you the correct gauge*

GAUGE: Pattern of (dc, ch 1) twice = 1"; 2 pattern rows = 1".

Note: Always work with right side facing you.

Starting at center bottom of bag with tango, ch 11. **1st rnd (right side):** Sc in 2nd ch from hook and in each of next 8 ch, work 4 sc in next (last) ch (one end of oval); working across opposite side of foundation chain, sc in each of next 8 ch, work 3 sc in next ch (24 sc); join with sl st to 1st sc. **2nd rnd:** Ch 1, work 2 sc in same place as sl st, sc in each of next 8 sc, 2 sc in each of next 4 sc, sc in each of next 8 sc, 2 sc in each of next 3 sc (32 sc); join. **3rd rnd:** Ch 1, work 2 sc in same place as sl st, 2 sc in next sc, sc in each of next 8 sc, 2 sc in each of next 8 sc, sc in each of next 8 sc, 2 sc in each of next 6 sc (48 sc); join. **4th rnd:** Ch 1, work 2 sc in each sc (96 sc); join.

5th rnd: Ch 4, skip 1st 2 sc, * dc in next sc, ch 1, skip 1 sc. Repeat from * around; sl st in 3rd ch of ch 4 to join (48 dc, counting turning ch). **6th rnd:** Ch 4, * dc in next dc, ch 1. Repeat from * around; join. Repeat 6th rnd 9 times more. Break off tango; attach parakeet.

16th rnd: Sc in each dc and ch-1 sp around (96 sc); join. **17th rnd:** Ch 1, sc in each sc around; join. Repeat last rnd once more with parakeet, then once with tango.

Repeat 5th rnd once, then repeat 6th rnd 10 times. Break off tango; attach parakeet. Repeat 16th rnd once; then repeat 17th rnd 3 times. Break off.

Strap: Insert two pins in top edge for location of strap ends. **1st row:** With parakeet sl st in 2 sc at 1 pin; crochet 25" chain, sl st in 2 sc at other pin; turn. **2nd row:** Sc in each ch across strap, sl st in next sc on last rnd of bag; turn. **3rd row:** Sc in each sc across strap, sl st in next sc on last rnd of bag. Break off.

Ties: With tango, sl st to sc midway between ends of strap along last rnd of bag, crochet 8" chain, sc in 2nd ch from hook and in each ch across, sl st in same place as sl st. Work another tie in same manner at opposite side of bag.

With tango crochet 8" chain, sl st to sc at center of bottom of bag; crochet 8" chain; sc in 2nd ch from hook and in each ch across. Break off. This forms dangling tassel.

General Directions

TO ENLARGE PATTERNS

You will need brown wrapping paper, pieced if necessary to make a large enough sheet for a pattern, a felt-tipped marker, pencil, and ruler. With pencil and ruler mark paper with a grid of 1", 2", or 4" squares (see indication on pattern) as follows: First, cut your paper into a true square or rectangle. Then mark dots 1", 2", or 4" apart (as marked on diagram) around edges, making the *same number* of spaces as there are squares around edges of pattern diagram. Form a grid by joining the dots across opposite sides of paper. Check to make sure you have the same number of squares as the diagram. With marker, draw in each square the same pattern lines you see in the corresponding square on the diagram. In this way your pattern will be enlarged to full size.

If you want to avoid the trouble of drawing a grid to enlarge your pattern, you can order a package of four 22" x 34" sheets of 1" graph paper for $1.20, postpaid, from Sewmakers, Inc., 1619 Grand Avenue, Baldwin, New York 11510.

ABBREVIATIONS AND TERMS USED FOR KNITTING AND CROCHETING

beg — beginning; ch — chain; cl — cluster; dc — double crochet; dec — decrease; dp — double-pointed; h dc — half double crochet; inc — increase; k — knit; lp — loop; p — purl; psso — pass slipped stitch over; rnd — round; sc — single crochet; sl — slip; sl st — slip stitch; sp — space; st — stitch; tog — together; tr — treble crochet; y o — yarn over.

* — **Asterisk** — means repeat instructions following asterisk as many times as specified, in addition to the first time.

[ ] — **Brackets** — indicate changes in size.

( ) — **Parentheses** — mean repeat instructions in parentheses as many times as specified.

Stockinette Stitch: K 1 row, p 1 row, or k each round if using circular or double-pointed needles.

Garter Stitch: K each row.

Credits

Designers

L. Cross, p. 85
Sally DeGaetano, 46, 107
M. L. Dreisbach, 58
Ann Foley, 172
E. Ginsberg, 95
Harriet Goldman, 11
Helen Hird, 148
Annette Hollander, 18
Zita Karas, 55
Sura Kayla, 102
Elizabeth D. Logan, 75
B. Muccio, 16, 78, 80
Pamela Negron, 104
T. Noda, 139
Charlotte Patera, 162, 167
Ruth Ramminger, 93
A. K. Roller, 14
Dina Schwartz, 154
Jo Smith, 111
Elizabeth Timmons, 64
Diane Wagner, 71
Marilyn Wein, 88, 150, 159
Woman's Day Staff, 27, 29, 32,
    50, 60, 83
M. L. Zanco, 98

Photographers

Frances McLaughlin Gill, p. 93
Sigrid Owen, 118, 119, 120, 121,
    145, 148, 150, 154, 162
Carmen Schiavone, 172
Woman's Day Studio, 11, 15, 16,
    18, 23, 27, 29, 32, 34, 46, 50, 55,
    58, 60, 64, 71, 75, 78, 80, 83, 85,
    88, 95, 98, 102, 104, 107, 111,
    139, 159, 167

57446